evermore

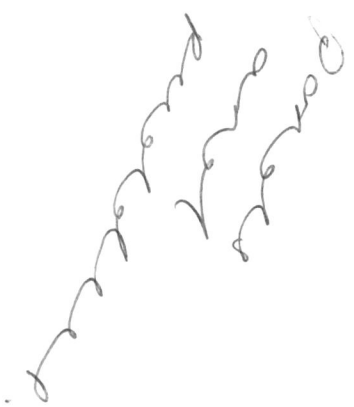

Compiled by

Ravens Quoth Press

Evermore Fourth Edition
Copyright © 2024 The Ravens Quoth Press
First published in Australia in October 2024 by The Ravens Quoth Press

Cover design by The Ravens Quoth Press
Formatting by Kara Hawkers
Editing by Kara Hawkers and E. Mery Blake

PENSIVE REFLECTIONS

Balm
Dream

EDGAR ALLAN POE-INSPIRED COLLECTION

Evermore

ROMANCE COLLECTION

Cherish
Tempest

GENERATIONS COLLECTION

TFW: Gen-Z Poetry

CHARITY COLLECTION

Shards: Mental Health Awareness

EDITOR'S CHOICE COLLECTION

Psythur

INDIVIDUAL COLLECTIONS

*Songs of the Underland & Other Macabre Machinations
by Kurt Newton*

Don't Cry on Cashmere by Brianna Malotke

The World Eats Love by Carol Edwards

The Secret Beautiful by Ximena Escobar

Follow us at:
linktr.ee/TheRavensQuothPress

"In their grey visions they obtain glimpses of eternity, and thrill, in awakening, to find that they have been upon the verge of the great secret."

—*Eleonora* by Edgar Allan Poe

GREG PATRICK A dual citizen of Ireland and the States, Greg Patrick is an Irish-Armenian traveller poet and the son of a Navy man. Also, a son of the Traveling People, he is a former humanitarian aid worker who worked with great horses for years. He loves the wilds of Connemara and Galway in the rain where he has written many stories. Greg spent his youth in the South Pacific and Europe and currently resides in Galway, Krakow, and sometimes the States. He now writes and travels.

Raven's Night

By Greg Patrick

"Deep into that darkness peering, long I stood there wondering, fearing, Doubting, dreaming dreams no mortals ever dared to dream before; But the silence was unbroken, and the stillness gave no token, And the only word there spoken was the whispered word"
-Edgar Allan Poe

Like a breathless emissary of night, haggard after a long journey to bear tidings, the dark poet faltered at last. Swaying like a pendulum tolling the hour, yet commenced his shuffling walk. Like a soloist by a solitary gas lamp's apparitional spotlight packing his case for the profitless walk back home. It was as if the restless shadows were granted form and face to mingle with the passerby. The gaunt apparition that once commanded a striking presence in the centre of candle-lit readings with the mystique of a famed conjurer or illusionist now reduced to dishevelled emaciation. He seemed strayed from the haunted pages of his stories. Raven hair maned a lion's stare. A bard's eyes like the lion's vision transcending the dark. His enigmatic profile seemed to hold watch over the night, a guardian of shepherdless dreams and holding sway over nightmares as shadows thronged him like an admiring public after the end of his story.

He was Atlas when the day broke and Orion when the night cast its dark spell, left to songs only the midnight scribe will dare tell. Huntsman's return, bard's sojourn, like a ghost march 'til dawn. His hand of the night scribe likewise beckoned at the few stars yet visible through the city lights like a pilgrim asking for an enlightenment just beyond his reach, as if snatching at their vigil candles, claw-like, talon-like some falling raptor that could not seize the bright quarry in the water far below but could not stop his falling for it.

Now hovering between worlds, like the voyage of a ghost vessel drifting between shores. Snow fell around him in ethereal splendour, like frozen tears or the hailing of a dark prince; a rightful heir of shadow returned, in a crystalline tribute, the frost glistening in the dark mane of his hair, like an ethereal crown.

He seemed like the apprentice of a sage or something wild pacing a night cage, one who revisits his master after being sent on a search for wisdom and was posed the question: what have you learned then in your travels of wisdom or foolishness?

The forbidding urban labyrinth with such evident squalor seemed an eerie dreamscape. The towering structures like misshapen sculptures glowered like dark idolatry. And to a sleepless brightness like the stars themselves and restless mind, the stream of consciousness and words flowed like the night tides stirred by the moon.

He seemed to glide rather than stride, with the air of a penniless prince humbled by circumstance, his ragged coat hems whispering on the stones like a flightless falcon crutching on broken wings though casting a shadow before him of a falcon soaring in slow motion as if guided by an elusive dream of restoration.

Sleepwalker, though profoundly conscious, of the restless dreamscapes of the heart. The squalor of the slums he roamed, like the ruins of a lost city, were unnerving to behold. The sunken-cheeked begged for alms in the shadow of the dilapidated soot-tarnished walls. Its uncouth denizens that congregated in circles by the patches of lights now when night fell, laughed in crude mirth as if to keep the dark and foreboding at bay as he passed them like a dark rumour whispered between them, a shadow of their own world passing them by.

He staggered, blinking into the beams of streetlamps, through the intervals of spectral light and shadow like a dream transcending the chords of a dream catcher unhindered. The beams like moonlight filtering through the dark canopy of a petrified jungle. Like a spectre drifting through worlds and a succession of dark thresholds.

A bewitchingly composed nocturne slipping through the harp strings. He seemed a dark tear of midnight wavering against the moon. It wasn't the voids but the fulfilment that made him seek the solace of the night. Man and moon in two solitudes. Like the first hesitant note of a masterpiece by a sleepless composer so haunting in its tone so as to seem a flight of ravens drawn by a stage conjurer's hand.

Every author leaves with a story untold and his soulful gaze, like a dwindling candle flame, seemed to delve the surrounding darkness for some image like listening to an endearment whispered to the night.

Every poet had a muse and the rare huntsman of the art through the poorly lit dreamscapes of the heart can seek the perfect words, but to truly find poetry is in that elusive vision was at last Poe's gift and curse. It seemed the end was written before a worthy beginning, its story ghost-written. He found her like a pilgrimage to beauty enshrined. The sleepless brightness of the midnight scribe began to be consumed by the darkness as if enveloped in ravens' wings. As if the shadow reclaimed its own. The embrace of a long-lost friend.

"Nevermore."

His dark eyes and betrayed, yearning sighs, brimming with stories yet untold welling with dark tears of an author who confronts what man secretly fears. Heir to shadow and successor to a lightless dawn. Soulful gaze like dwindling candle flame seemed to delve into the surrounding darkness for some image, like listening for a dark rumour whispered to the night.

He raised his glass like a toast to the stars. Like a champion of darkness mortally wounded he seemed to stride for a final confrontation with the awaiting light and it seemed even with the sensation of falling in slow motion as the intoxicating bottle fell like an hourglass and he after it to the cold night's bower.

"Nevermore."

He crumpled, like the page of a rejected manuscript by his own hand, then cast aside. His words failed him as he failed her…

He fell then as if in slow motion, silhouetted against the moon like a teardrop of midnight down the face of a stone angel watching over the night.

Passerby hastened by him to escape the cold in phantasmal procession. None paused for him. The hansom carriages clattered by and still he lingered as the snow swept over him softly. The chill wind like a parting caress to his dwindling senses. The steeple bell tolled the hour. His hour. He seemed drawn down by skeletal hands…then…

As the dark melody of the chill wind, like the parting caress of an underworld goddess through his hair, took voice and form. It seemed a tender hand soothed his cheek and only then he dared look up…

He at last beheld her, mirage to a nomad's eyes, as if she waited for him in the dusk…

"Annabel Lee…"

Rose on Poe's Grave

By Greg Patrick

"I wish I could write as mysteriously as a cat"
-Edgar Allan Poe

The door was blown ajar, papers tossed with red leaves as if by a yearning sigh of the chill Autumn wind, opened as if by the bidding of a Gemini of two golden eyes that seemed ignited by spectral moonlight that filtered through the door. It was as if a presence materialising at the threshold illuminated the dark, lithe form of a black cat curled like a dark question mark by the hearth.

As if in answer to that question mark poised, it was as if the shadows massing at the door and the restless shadows of those hastening as midnight tolled from the steeples of Baltimore, were granted form, a face by the maleficence of its eyes—eyes that mirrored a haggard, gaunt figure.

Like a maddeningly elusive muse summoned or conjured by a sleepless composer's inspiration, with the languid grace of a nocturne's notes the cat rose and floated over to the author who swept in haggard and dishevelled from the harsh elements as if ushering in the night, like an emissary of nightmare behind haunted eyes.

His garments flourished like raven wings around a slain warrior propped up in the aftermath, like a scarecrow over a barren harvest of ghosts. The impossibly golden huntress eyes of the cat at vigil missed nothing in the dark except for his presence in monochromed vision.

"Endor!" He beamed.

He smiled seldom but always did for her.

His black cat.

His resonant tone betrayed weariness as his gaze did old scars, like a lion's purr in the primal dark. A trembling chill palm caressed its soft darkness in passing, the way a Stradivarius note would to the sense of a brooding audience member in an opera hall.

Like the echo of a soloist's violin player, the cat answered the gentle voice, soft as the sound of moths emerging from cocoons past metamorphosis, like debutantes emerging in pale frills to seek out killing lights waiting in the night. Poe's eyes, like a fireless hearth brooding darkly, were kindred to the cat's eyes, vision beheld through the dark.

Eyes that transcended the darkness in which men sought the shadow sanctuary to cry like prisoners in an oubliette, tears brimming like ink particles falling on a page, seeing through the darkness while other eyes remained oblivious. A kindred searcher's eyes, perceiving all things that meant to hide in darkness and behind masks.

He heard what was only confided to the night, like the sigh of disappointment at the threshold's closed door. Haunted eyes beamed as they searched for the right words as one would an elusive keepsake or ring in the dreamscape of snow, or looking for footprints leading the way past the stately homes and apparitional spotlight cast by gas lamps, promising mystery with each step. Past the window where a solitary figure stands alone on Christmas eve more boxes left under trees than people to open them. Eyes meet the walker's outside before turning away to steel oneself till dawn or cock a revolver and look one last time to the night.

Meeting eyes alone outside of cat or stranger with his writing. Seeing lovers meet in secret, circles of thuggish men whispering in a circle plotting.

One stands aloof from it all before the mullioned window of his muse like a caroller before a darkened window as the snow begins to fall, and only the passing of a horse-drawn carriage breaks his melancholic reverie and he is tossed a rose in passing by a gloved hand from the coach leaving him with a lasting sense of mystery at what enigmatic stranger would grace him thus. And he could linger so long that the rose would fall like a glacial ornament on the cobbles.

All the night is a story…

Just shadows in the night to the eyes of the cat and writer delving into its danse macabre of mysteries. The cat tenses before appearing on the windowsill next to the poet writing by dwindling candlelight as if listening outside to the words in the serenade of the wind. The gaze he casts in a love song to the darkness is like a dark nomad's eyes gazing at his reflection in a night oasis and to the stars as he sighs in duet with the fall wind and winter in his soul.

"What tidings then from the night, huntress?" the poet asks as he lifts the windowsill as if to an emissary arrived from the night to a lone prince's throne room.

He gathers the cat fondly in his arms and bears her to the warmth of the hearthside, before sinking wearily to his author's chair like that of a midnight scribe, like a battle-weary prince into a dark throne of a cursed house, listening to a rebel angel as bard for a mortal musician cannot bring the celestial fires of the stars to light the page or inflame the dark of a warrior's soul in dark raven's wings enveloping immortal words at a song.

"I wish I could write as mysteriously as a cat..." he mused and yearned.

And to a life that afforded little happiness but by a pen that séanced ghosts as if by a stage illusionist's conjuring hand to haunt the imagination. He had thought prayer was little more than talking to air, but as if in reply to a black cat's stare, the night answered in unexpected ways for those who sleepwalk the poorly lit dreamscapes of the heart.

And he opened his eyes to a blank page in the same way a black cat's eyes beheld a lone figure appearing from the cold night at the threshold as if summoned standing against a chill background of snow falling like ghost tears for a dark past.

He sighed as if in ventriloquism to the night wind and looked into the hearth flames, 'til they shone with their own fires and began to write anew as sworn scribe of the night's boundless mysteries.

Song for the Raven Queen

By Greg Patrick

"You have witchcraft in your lips"-William Shakespeare

You were night to me—starless darkness in its gothic majesty, in all its sacred mystery—ruling hearts like a princess of legend and history. Night by which one counts on crushing brink of sea as ever Poe wrote of Annabelle Lee.

You were darkness crowned in midnight, so it was your face suspended in magic moment and night. So effortlessly did you mingle with night itself so as to haunt each dream after and all to the fate's laughter.

Mirage before me like the desert stars to a nomad's eyes that shone me on...smile like a song one could not get out of one's head. Smile that was silence set to nocturne, too magical to be magic and to be anything but a work of possession to a composer not of inspiration and at the touch all the night's sensations brought like a dark bard to a dark prince enthroned to sing ballads unsung of Guinevere's incarnation.

Poetry in the flourish of raven waves like tidings borne to the stars and it was all crossed out in the stars as if by the cards, surrounded by magic, as many roles in triumph and tragic...haunted as if by the conspiring fates taunted, cast spell of night so long that it was my own shadow before me.

The nightmare that passed the dreamcatcher's net for all the hauntings of midnight-crowned regret like something too wild to be held by a snare. Dream to banish nightmare. Nightmare to banish dream and for every promise of a new start, every smile behind Endorian eyes an illusionist art, like a procession of carts, bearing each warrior fallen—till the carriage to the night castle awaited.

The palace with night-blossoming roses in every vine, and nights of candles and wine have vanished with the dawn, and only ruins appear—even abandoned by ghosts to be haunted by the living and it seemed a toast to Poe's grave was all that was left to be giving.

I had dared dream it was to be a duet to the muse, but it was merely a slow-burning fuse, sung by one in a cowl and by its song the fates answered smile with vindictive scowl.

Turned away by the one I was told not to see again, so that when I dared look back with Orphean yearning after one gone with no trace, truth stood in awkward contrast to an illusionist's deceptive grace. It was to face as many dawns with only a shadow haunting my step, as I walk to the midnight train, and if I was stabbed on the way, at least I would have slept.

Like Banquo's ghost he appears, as if hailed by falling raven feathers like midnight tears…stranger at his own wake. His step falters as if from dark eye's spell and intoxication begins to stagger…the cold tangible as a dagger, disoriented by shock of words; lion trampled by the herds.

Words lost like a message in a bottle on dark waves tossed. Doppelganger of a soul lost. Lost soul, somnambulant to the bell's toll. Jostled by the herds, just another face to the passerby, like a hungry beast after all that glitters in a world deaf to a thousand heartbeats, ventriloquised in a soloist song to be heard? In a dying ruin of a world, that would barter the heart in fool's gold, as if love could be sold, but gone as if banished like children of gaudy displays before the red lances of the sun's rays.

The streets silent now, as silent as when we had to ourselves…that night under the Tinseltown lights and the night never felt so cold. What streets then are these? Galway? Derry? Baltimore…? Does it matter anymore…? Awkward truth had stood before the graceful art of deception. Left only with the programme of the night. The man of honour—Poe.

His eyes seemed to delve into the soul—eyes envision scenes of his stories—of vengeance and Haunting glories. Our eyes meet with startling recognition in the street… Those unmistakable eyes, streaked dark over a stone angel's face that into eternity cries. Ghosts you see are the more haunted by mortals and there we stood framed in mirrors like ghosts silhouetted by magic portals.

Pale face like a ghostly witness to unredressed wrong, who is anyone to think themselves strong? In spirit I lift him from the snow where has fallen, like a toast of cognac to the night and a black rose to the grave of my own dream. Like Azrael I appear. Dark suit like broken wings, like a ghost dance brave's shroud to dream fated to die, because I had no true place as myself, a guardian of the old ways and I must leave or die and forsake the dark rose. And where in that shell is the great master of prose? Toasted by cognac and rose to a grave before a dark shrine to a dark prince's ghost that fell and rose.

Where in the beggar turned away from the door and a chair's place was the dark prince of poetry that ruled fear in stories told through the centuries by the charmed flames of the hearthplace, aloof from new and the mad race? In spirit I lift him from the snow and bear him away…to a safe house he knows. And then I realise at the shrill of the midnight trains that I had really picked myself up as if raised on dark wings, one left by the Valkyrie to rise for another night and battle for it is not the lot of the lion to be trampled by cattle. A gambler's queen of hearts, to a king of hearts last gamble, dealing hearts one could never win back. Was it in the cards all along…?

After the bewitchment of song, lips like reopening wounds. But the heart will not be lulled to an elusive repose and wounds will not close…the spell has taken hold…haunted by the song of the black rose. No, it was not a Hollywood ending, but if there is finally a warrior worth killing than there is a heart worth rending.

The deceptive painted desert of tinsel town carried on obliviously in its endless rush, its sound and its fury…. You paid homage to one outcast poet, Poe. And what I wished of him I wish of you…that I could have found you where you were left broken and lifted you up from the cold street, as your song and words uplifted a heart that was downtrodden on an avenue of stars.

And I'd like to think you are there now above the rush and roar, the hatred, illness and fear, where we cannot see the stars anymore above the starless veil of the city lights. No paper would offer you homage yet for all that there were nights, I wish I could have renamed every constellation in the sky after you, every vision of goddesses testing the heart of mortals, every dragon and wild thing unleashed at mortals to test the sharpness of their wit and blade.

Those constellations enshrined in symmetries of eternal fire, gleaming in the uncertain eyes of sleepless warriors on eve of battle, inspiring and rallying hearts with their distant light and legend, all but Orion, eternal castaway for that shared story and moment under city-obscured stars. Remembered above statues and red carpets, even as the world under them changed and changed again, till their names were called mythology and humanity itself became a myth and still dared wield the muse and power of the old goddesses it seemed, casting that dark spell over any who stopped to listen.

I think of the black rose I once gave you and its whispered caveat, don't hold on then too tightly. Let go, the blood is showing through your finger. *Keep to the pen instead, when I go into the night, you can't follow this time...* There was a mercy in that warning that I didn't understand then and maybe I don't now. I remember when we left the theatre together the streets were quiet as if a dark stage was set.

We talked and laughed and said goodnight. I lingered then as your car drove away in the darkness closed my eyes, immersed in that darkness as if enfolded in a dark angel's wings, dreaded by some, revered by a few, there is a solace to that majestic darkness where rebels are allowed the heresy of tears and the defiance of dreams, and I dared to look back with Orphean valediction...not wanting it to be true.

.

The Witching Hour: An Evening with Edgar Allan Poe

By Greg Patrick

The rejected manuscript was crumpled in a cold hand that seemed to beckon forth the

cold of the winter night that cast its restless dark spell over the cobblestone streets.

One would have thought him a ghost if not betrayed, as living by a sigh that

steamed like a smoking revolver in the cold air.

On the solitary return to his lodging from the publisher's Edgar passed in a half-ambulant

way the gabled houses pausing at last in the stream of more gentile passerby letting the

carriages pass and top-hatted gents and belles flow like an oblivious human stream

for one who was somnambulant to his own dark dreamscape.

More shadow than man displaced by light and traded like a dark rumour between

sentinel-like lampposts in vigil like guardians of night clad in black armour that parted

ways as if ranks allowing a wounded prince to pass through. He passed thus as if a dark

tear flowing through vision or as a fleeting yet haunting and enflamed inspiration through

his psyche.

Passing like a dark rumour or jest traded between night guardsmen in the cold.

Like a fickle moth making rounds between fatal brightnesses. Frozen tears of lovelorn

desire for one above his station clung to his cheek smeared like war paint on his pale

countenance and swaying in intoxication like a stilted lamplighter igniting the gas lamps in

the twilight.

Like a haggard nigh emaciated scarecrow upon whom an aura of unbanished darkness

clung like a raven and like that messenger of night, he seemed emissary with words for a

queen's ear. He was lured like the moths that haunted his sleepless candlelight nights at

the pen where he wrote like a midnight scribe. Moths he trapped in empty cups and he

released like toasts to the night. He was lured by a dangerous radiance as he drew close to a

masque societal ball for the debutantes of Baltimore high society. The darkness pressed too

close…

Like a proud monarch scorning a fawning court of shadows or an aloof lover

shrugging off a dark temptress, he resisted the pull to fall in the snow, for his eyes beheld

like a pilgrim's vision through its spectral shimmer the angelic beckoning. As if a princess

bidding a black knight arise from his knees. Gaze as craving as an alms seeker in its

entreaty cast like the last card towards one who he beheld descended from a hansom

carriage unescorted. The night itself seemed to sigh with the selfsame homage of a black

knight to a fair queen and snow fell like a hailing tribute of pale gold. The very essence of a

poet's inspiration if ever one was truly inspired.

It was as if a sleepless artist standing helpless before a blank canvas saw the image of

masterpiece project in fast-forward upon the awaiting canvas and eyes could but trace the

movements in symmetry of dream and then for it to fade like a snow angel.

She appeared

ephemeral as a mirage to a nomad's eyes, glittering as an oasis. Like a poem written against

the light before passing into the hall with a melting dematerialising quality of

an apparitional and likewise the pale plumed horses that drew the coach appeared

phantom-like…dream-like. In a flourish of gossamer and silk, she passed his sight into the

music-filled hall as if a princess returning to the bardic songs in which she had strayed.

Presentable he was…passably so to clear the doorman's scrutiny. An invitation fallen in the

snow held up like a king of heart's card and face composed poker-like.

He paused at the threshold, lingering, like ardent words of admiration at the lips.

Eyes blinking from the darkness.

His shadow cast ominously upon the guests before making entrance. There was

something inexplicably lordly in his bearing for all his haggard and gaunt appearance.

"*Mr Poe,*" he heard it whispered—something like awe in the tone.

"The writer…"

All were masked, the guests and liveried servants, only for him.

It was the way he wrote and lived. In writing as in life, his was not the masquerade.

Like an emissary of darkness, like the enigmatic raven of his poem, he approached his

muse.

Gowned in resplendence, she stood in solitary splendour. So fair to behold that none dared

ask her to dance. Hair like a crowning of beauty in celestial gold in cascading wavelets

spilt over the mask she wore like champagne spilling in endless slow motion. The crowd

parted as if making way for a dark bard who had a song for his queen. Everyone else in the

room faded to mere silhouettes or the shadows of charmed serpents swaying to the

Endorian maleficence of music that ceased, and the dancers unclasped gloved hands bowed

and applauded. The dance floor was vacant.

He whispered to a Stradivarius-player, who nodded and turning some pages. The musical

notes were like a spell book's incantations as he took up his instrument. Yet the writer

heard not the song no matter how beautiful it's strains before a smile

that was silence set to music and presence like a nomad or mariner's star set in the dark of

night.

Their eyes met like a duet of nocturne and aria and he bowed like a courtier spellbound

with her as readers were with his stories.

"May I have this last dance before midnight? Only my Lady... Take off the mask if you

will..."

For ours is ever the witching hour when darkness has its own sway. The moment I knew

enchantment at a glanced and it would not go unsung with an homage to darkness.

He didn't feel the dance floor... He only felt alive. The candle flames became stars one could

not see in the city nights. The bells toll midnight then jarringly with the waking shock of a

dream interrupted, yet they danced through it as others took off their masks and no less the

moment of startling recognition between them. A poet alone with the vision of his

inspiration.

He raised the gloved hand to his lips, his eyes never leaving hers. In the same way his

haunted insatiably thirsty eyes looked over the rim of a cup in a toast to beauty in the

swaying intoxication of blue eyes before seeking to extinguish the vexing fire of inspiration

to its last smouldering embers.

In those arms encircling like frail moth wings forsaking the fatal allure of earthbound

Lantern lights and instead sought the stars and in feeling so the sensation of flight.

"When will I see you again, for I've not beheld your like and my dreams and definition of

beauty will never be the same?" Poe wondered.

I will see you and know you again when next I compose and in a golden

mirage when I fall in the snow with vision purged of the time you cross the dancefloor and

aisle without me. For a lost soul cannot find his way past the dark without an angel's hand.

THE RAVENS QUOTH PRESS

LINDA SPARKS is a poet/author primarily in the horror genre. She prefers writing horror poetry as she is not afraid of the dark. Linda served as Editor for *Valkyrie Magazine*. She has several novels published and has been published in multiple anthologies. She lives in Floriday.

The Pit and the Pendulum

By Linda Sparks

I was tightly bound and secured by the web of a dream

As I gave thoughts to the grave and my imprisoned scream.

The madness and the brutal memory of my bruises came

Insolently creeping into this moment of torture and pain.

My inquisitor had bled me well, seeking forbidden things,

That I might cry out just as a dying man's soul sings.

In that last moment, between breath and heartbeat,

Is the final release truly a promise of relief so sweet?

My vision is aghast, as there is absolutely nothing to see

But blackness and unknown horror and gruesome eternity.

I know well I am condemned to a death so grim

In Toledo, this place of terror and nightmare grins.

The judges are above having delivered my fate

With no one to save me, as it was all far too late.

The floor beneath was treacherous with slime and mould,

And clammy, decayed fungus and vapours so brutally cold.

I had dared to step forward in treacherous movement,

Shocked to find myself at the horrid edge of a deep pit.

I might easily have slipped and crushed my head

And most certainly, their prisoner would be quite dead.

Water and small amounts of food were given to me

And I drank with great thirst and ate the meat lustily.

It seemed I was not yet being meant to starve away.

They had other ideas about how they planned to play.

Agitation of spirit kept me awake and all I could not see.

Yet sleep drowned me as this body is prime mortality.

When I awakened, I saw Time holding a pendulum in hand.

Dread coiled within me as I guessed what they had planned.

And now I was bound securely, watching the pendulum's sweep.

With each movement stronger, sharper, and sequentially deep.

The motions began as brief, provocative and measured.

I held my breath between sweeps as my life was treasured.

To and fro, with easy, consistent sharp-edged charm.

The massive pendulum warned me of its great harm.

Judges watched from above with slithering, smiling faces

As the swinging scimitar shifted through its powerful paces.

Rats with ravenous red eyes stalked from the black night,

Eager to observe that promised finale, and odious fright.

I knew well, they would fight over my flesh and bones

And care nought for my shrill screams and bitter moans.

Or would the slice of that cruel blade slash my heart

And release me swiftly into that bloodily dead part?

Could I truly aspire to accept this possible end?

Already having observed the death of a friend?

The blade's vibration increased and the swish of air

As it swept above me, ripping my garment there.

With horror, I watched it slowly descend each sweep

And I laughed with joy and howled and tried to weep.

The edge of the massive blade was razor sharp

Hissing with maddening music of an angel harp.

This grotesque dungeon was to be my grave

As no voices rose for me or tried to save.

It came to me in a moment of ultimate madness so fine,

I shivered at the cleverness of my potential design.

Taking the remnant of the spicy meat, I rubbed it well

Upon those bands that secured me in this living hell.

I howled with anger and the agony of despair

Knowing well the rodents would not even care.

Yet they moved quickly to taste the beef

Severing my bonds with their sharp teeth.

Now I understood as I escaped the blade's kill

The abyss of the pit was eagerly awaiting me still.

Shouts and screams, perhaps of rage, and defeat

Rose in the air as rats were deceived by the meat.

And I was free but still a dead man after all

Looking down into the pit, and ready to fall.

As I moved forward, eyes wide open with alarm,

I stepped off and a strong one grabbed my arm.

General Lasalle was now here in the Toledo city.

He and his army had ultimately come to rescue me..

Murder of Poe

By Linda Sparks

Edgar Allan was just a man like any other

A boy raised sadly without his loving mother.

He followed a path quite unknown to men

Writing Gothic, mysteries, macabre and sin.

Marrying his 13-year-old cousin too

Who died so young and brought him rue.

The torment that filled dearest "Eddy"

Flowed like a dark river's sombre eddy.

Concise and sharp was his wit

As he reviewed a piece of lit.

This caused jealousy and anger too

And enemies that tried to leave no clue.

Intoxicated, choleric, diabetic or drugged

Or possibly cooped in voting or even mugged.

Those filled with hate wrote of his dark fate

Caring little for the truth or whether it was late.

Poe's words spoke for themselves and outlived time

With his short stories and masterful poetry and rhyme.

A man brilliant beyond anyone's belief

Yet doomed to die a cruel death sans relief.

Oh, how they hated the man and smeared him well,

Calling him a drunkard, druggie and a man in hell.

But the truth be told in this tragic tale at last,

Edgar Allan Poe's honour and fame are forever cast.

Young daughters sit by their father's knee

Listening to the greatest Poet ever to be.

.

Sepulchre by the Sea

By Linda Sparks

Oh, come with me, my love, and feel the tears of the sea,

Splash across our pallid faces and expunge our agony.

Heed thee the whisper of the siren's alluring song,

Enchanting my soul and heart all the night long.

The sea salt upon my tongue is bittersweet and mild,

And the roaring desire within my corpse is ever wild.

I lie abed in the carven rock awaiting your eyes

Hauntingly beautiful luminous stars in the skies.

Violent storms lash against this ancient rock and stone,

And bitterly, I am suffering and longing for you alone.

How is it that I have found myself cognisant and awake?

Am I a vampire that urgently requires a cardiac stake?

Or is it just a maddened dream that fills my head?

Is it truly possible that I have found myself dead?

Graves and tombs and mausoleums are my fate

Being entombed in this sepulchre, it is far too late

For me to kiss your sensuous, angelic face.

I rage against this cold and stony seaside place.

Will angels come to me and sing their song,

And forgive my life's errors and all my wrong?

Or shall I lament like the siren's wailing voice,

Because I am shrouded here without a choice?

The lullaby of the soothing tide urges me to sleep.

I struggle valiantly, but my wandering soul is deep.

I hear the night tides and sorrowful rue

Wishing only to be alive again with you.

.

The Black Cat

By Linda Sparks

I loved animals, and my disposition was mild
Docility and humility and not at all a bit wild.
I wed early and my wife was sweet and kind
And we both loved animals, similar in mind.
Our home was filled with numerous pets:
Goldfish, dogs, rabbits and we had no regrets.
I encountered a fine black cat with beautiful eyes.
Some thought ebon felines were witches in disguise.
I bequeathed this black cat Pluto as his name
Roman god of the underworld and evil fame.
How could I possibly expect this curse?
When I merely enjoyed poetic verse?
Alas, I began to follow the darkest path
Fuelled by alcohol, which inspired my wrath.
My ill temper grew, and cruelty began to rise;
The drink led me to brutality and things unwise.
My wife felt the pain of this evil as well
And for the animals, it became a living hell.
Somehow, the vile drink inspired a beast within me,

And the animals were injured and treated with cruelty.

Even my wife tried to avoid the back of my hand,

Because she could not quite imagine or understand

How I had become this beast rather than a man

Even though these deeds had never been my plan.

Then came the terrible day when I made her cry

When I viciously tortured Pluto and removed his eye.

Now with this terrible affliction, the cat fled from me,

And my anger flared, never blaming my own brutality.

This creature with his hideous eye, filled me with dread

So, I formed a noose and slipped it around his dark head.

With ease I hung this loving, beautiful cat

And smiled, thinking that was the end of that.

As the black creature swung from the tree,

I was bursting with an ominous, horrid glee.

My relief that the loving cat was now gone,

Made me drink deeply and burst into song.

Disgust, bitterness, relief and dread of the beast

Yet I wished to call for a lavish celebratory feast.

Perverseness is a primitive impulse of a human heart,

And I refused to accept any blame for my ignoble part.

I desired to commit wrong even with tears in my eyes,

Hanging the creature from the gallows, I knew was unwise.

I knew this immortal sin could jeopardise my soul
And in my wickedness that appeared to be my goal.

On the night of the cruel deed being undertaken,
A cry of fire was enough for us to luckily awaken.

After the fire, a strange and singular image did appear,
The image of a cat with a noose which caused my fear.

As months passed by, the phantasm of the cat's death,
Seemed to frazzle me and often it took away my breath.

I thought to find another cat to try to ease my pain,
A black cat arrived except his breast was not the same.

A patch of white filled his breast with purity
Truly protecting against any imagined iniquity.

The animal easily chose to accompany me home,
Undoubtedly, he had been previously on the roam.

The creature revealed great fondness for me
But I was disgusted out of some perversity.

This monster had also lost an eye in some odd way,
And this endeared him to my wife the very first day.

As my aversion began to grow, the cat loved me more,
Such that I could not bear its loathsome eyesore

As though I had a hand in torturing this one too
And its gaping orbit was a reminder of my rue.

For in truth, I had no regret at all for my grievous sin
And knew my soul well I would do the killing again.
One day in the cellar I raised the axe to slay the beast
And my wife stayed my hand and asked me to cease.
With a terrible rage, I buried the axe within her head
And without even a moan, upon the spot, she fell dead.
I determined the best way for the body to hide
Was to be walled up in the cellar and inside.
With great care, I plastered the fireplace well
Such that not a soul asking could even tell.
When the police arrived, I felt calm and cool,
Knowing how easy that I could manage to fool.
With a sinister smile upon my face,
I allowed them to search the place.
A frightful howl and shriek filled the air;
And they began pulling bricks from there.
It seemed the hideous demon cat was inside
With the decaying corpse and I would be tried
For the death of my innocent and peaceful love
Soon dangling from the hangman's noose above.

.

The Masque of the

Red Death

By Linda Sparks

Thousands lay dying in the streets without sorrow

Their bodies bloated and rotting far beyond the morrow.

The Avatar of blood had claimed them one and all

Dying in crimson quicker than they could even fall.

The Red Death killed with innocuous speed

Slaying all, regardless of their rank or creed.

Yet Prince Prospero deemed to lock himself away

In an extravagant abbey where he could be gay.

Leaving behind half a dead kingdom in the street,

Prospero gathered a thousand to have a merry meet.

Extravagant food and luscious wine to fill the time,

As the black ebony clock loudly voiced its chime.

Ballet dancers, musicians, buffoons and more

And with singing and dancing and gaiety galore.

The iron gates were welded securely against pain,

Allowing none to ingress or egress ever again.

Prospero was arrogantly assured they would all survive

Once the plague had finally abated, and they were alive.

With songs being sung and laughter, most high

The prince and his friends had no reason to cry.

Through the seven rooms of colour, they did dance,

Feeling gay and revelling wildly as though in a trance.

One night, the prince had come up with a brilliant plan,

That his guests would masquerade and smile behind a fan,

Or obscured by a masque where they might smile

And easily hide their wicked desires and their guile.

Each reveller donned a beautiful masque and cloak

Whispering their secrets like maddened folk.

They swept through the rooms of green and blue,

Purple, white, and luxurious lush violet too.

Each room blazed with the colour and windowpane

Filtered similar colours, yet some thought him insane.

Was he truly mad, or would they dare to touch him?

Just to see if there was insanity or gaiety within?

It mattered little as they waited for the clock to chime,

Marking the hour, stopping the music, stopping time.

Music and dancers halted in a mysterious thrall,

As the clock counted the hour at the masquerade ball.

One of the seven rooms was not quite the same.

Morbid black and crimson windowpanes.

Did it hold some secret destiny for all?

Or just a dark, grotesque room for a ball?

As the ebony clock began to strike the mid of night,

The revellers were frozen in place in their eerie fright.

They had not noted a mysterious masquerade guest

Who wore graveclothes and decay upon his chest.

Terror ascended as this guest depicted the Red Death.

All who gazed upon his grim visage held their breath.

The prince was enraged at this grotesque mask

And yelled "Who Dares?" this monstrous task.

He called out his men to capture the wicked one,

So, he might hang him under the morning sun.

But none came forth to seize the dark one

And with dagger in hand, Prospero did run.

And then he saw the face of true death

And dropped to the floor without breath.

Others clamoured and tried to seize the one.

But found his graveclothes were void and done.

As they cried out in terror and fell to the floor,

Knowing the end of their lives forever more.

And the ebony clock did not strike again

At the Red Death's victorious leering grin.

.

The Fall of the House of Usher

By Linda Sparks

Upon invitation I came to visit my melancholy mate

Even though I'd not seen him in many years of late.

When I arrived at the decrepit house I felt insufferable gloom.

A manse in disrepair and friend with eyes as wild as a loon.

Roderick Usher had greatly altered now with vacant eyes

And nervous agitation and I feared that my visit was unwise.

During our boyhood days, we were comrades, but that is all

And I never expected to receive this bleak hand-written call.

Usher revealed mental idiosyncrasies that I noted well

And physical maladies which spoke of his private hell.

He was cadaverous with large, luminous, liquid eyes,

And pallid lips that spoke softly and then uttered cries.

Hair wild and unheeded, emaciated and agitated of soul.

I could not grasp this was the sturdy boyhood lad of old.

And then I caught a glimpse of Lady Madeline, his twin,

And felt such rigours at the sight as she was ghastly thin.

She spoke not at all but moved wispily upon the stair

And yet I remembered her as once exceedingly fair.

A demon of fear began to crawl beneath my skin

And I wished to purge myself of any hidden sin.

Truly, this house and this grotesque domain

Was cause enough to make a man go insane.

And suddenly he announced she had died.

Was it even possible that Usher secretly cried?

I cannot say as not a tear dropped from his eye

Allegedly close as twins, I could not conceive why.

Usher stated he would now preserve her corpse a while

In a temporary tomb of barren cold and without style.

I tried to reason exactly why this oddity might be,

But my former friend had no wish to listen to me.

It was a fortnight she was sealed in a family vault,

Despite that, I tried to dissuade him from this fault.

Inexplicable vagaries of madness continued to alarm

And I truly feared my friend might do himself harm.

A violent storm screamed about the door

And Usher whispering "she is no more."

Then the ripping, tearing, insidious sounds began

And Usher's face progressed to cadaverously wan.

He listened for the sounds; his eyes as wild as death

And I totally anticipated seeing his very last breath.

At first the movements were feeble and weak

As though something undead was simply meek.

Then they grew in power, as might the fury of God

As the movements ripped and shuddered the sod.

There she swayed, bloodied white robes and torn nails,

Moving slowly yet with ire, leaving a crimson trail.

She was the sister twin born of the same mother,

And she fell brutally upon her shrieking brother.

Tearing him apart, ripping at his head and his face,

As the roof fell, the walls split, destroying the place.

Death agonies twisted and entwined the two

As pieces of the walls shattered and flew.

I cannot blame the violent, angry storm at all.

'Twas the undead sister's rage caused the fall..

The Craven

By Linda Sparks

Midnight whispered clearly, as I knew you loved me dearly.

Hours are long, and others sleep, and I and the dark belong

With the pen in my spidery hand, craven things at my command,

As easily these words slip from my head yet fill readers with dread.

Yet I hear the ravenous croak of a dark one without a cloak.

Is he what he seems or merely a madman's lucid dream?

Can it be a raven perched upon my chamber door?

Whispering salaciously and harshly, "nevermore."

I did not direct a true question here. My madness cannot be severe.

All I asked was a very simple thing. caring none for news you bring.

I wish to know exactly where we go as all men should know

After death arrives with his knife and severs my life.

The bird calmly implies that he is sordidly wise

And I avoid his dark eyes and smother my futile cries.

I attempted to silence my sorrow, praying for the morrow

Weeping in silence without surcease or suspense

Who could stymie this as I longed again for her kiss

But knew in death she lay and would forever there stay.

That whispered word unspoken was but an abysmal token.

My mind was viciously rent without the slightest relent.

I could not sleep but merely weep in pain

Never to see my lost Lenore ever again.

With pen and frenzied pain, I began to write again

Caring little for the wicked hour or the bird's glower.

He mocked me with his eyes and his eternal lies.

Leaving me without hope or prayer and in great despair.

Within my chamber, my soul was burning like a hot coal

Brightly blistering and scorching and ever torturing.

Yet the words screamed upon the page with my utter rage.

And more than ever, the bird needed a tether and an iron cage.

This ominous bird of gloom and doom haunted my room.

An ungainly stricken fowl, not as pure as the wisest owl

Of white feathers and fair weather nor the craven bird's scowl.

I know not who brought him here but my heart strikes with fear.

Birds do not enter a chamber door, never ever have before.

This creature speaks of horror and the breath of death

Stealing treacherously those memories I have left.

Why had he chosen me as prey to mock me this way?

Prophet bird or demon too? Bring me this horrific rue.

I cannot sink into sleep or languish in my grief and weep.

When a craven bird of yore boldly perches above my door.

Promising me my core of sorrow will be ever more.

The raven's beak stabbed my heart, keeping Lenore apart.

Did this fiend, or angels wild, carry away my beloved child?

Now I suffer my anguish and linger and languish

Seeing no end to this or the bird's horrendous hiss.

He croaks the words I hate at this hour so very late

And flees from me, leaving my chamber door ever more.

My bitter shadowed broken soul upon the tufted floor

The dark bird in flight taking my soul away evermore.

MARK ANDREW HEATHCOTE is adult learning difficulties support worker. He has poems published in journals, magazines, and anthologies both online and in print. He resides in the UK, and is from Manchester. Mark is the author of *In Perpetuity* and *Back on Earth*, two books of poems published by Creative Talents Unleashed.

Gazing Into the Abyss of Corruption

By Mark Andrew Heathcote

It's a precarious, insecure situation

gazing into the abyss of corruption.

Working like Sisyphus did and done

for no pleasure or recompense.

Sure, this is how it is working today.

No gains to bank or treasure.

Trying to roll that big rock up a mountain,

higher and higher, higher and higher,

only to watch it slide back down the other side

listening to the snickering of heartless fools.

Jackals that somehow get to stay on top?

While we all work like broken mules.

Living hand to mouth, hoping to survive

another winter cough, without funds

or heating fuel or even the money to send

our kids to their first elementary school.

Sure, they'll learn the cost of living

by walking there with holes in their shoes.

They'll even make dear old Sisyphus proud

how they, too, never cried aloud.

In a State of Rigor Mortis

By Mark Andrew Heathcote

We want to live life in a state of rigor mortis

But the world isn't dead, it's a living thing

It's got stuff we don't care to understand

And yet, it's a foreign entity to some of us

Who wants only to destroy or rebuild it?

That's where the real problem lies.

Try as we might, we can't hold the fabric of nature—

completely still. Like a pond spider on water,

because fauna and flora are not like that.

So, you weave a spell that has multiple facets.

But in all seriousness, verity doesn't stay stagnated

In all truth, nothing remains perpetually motionless.

The world is halfway through its infancy

Its setting has long been in the Regency period

A time of grandeur and fantasy

Our world is splintered in misogynistic lust

The world our mother is expressing her love,

As love often does when it turns to hate.

A Dark Shade of Grey

By Mark Andrew Heathcote

Look at the blue of his eyes.

What do you think they disguise?

Look, they're turning a dark shade of grey.

What do you think they disguise?

Look at his eyes. Do you think he cries?

Look at his eyes and how he hides.

What do you think they camouflage?

He's full of remorseless egocentric charms.

I guess he avoids the good in other people's eyes.

Look at his eyes. Look at his eyes.

They fan the flames of deceit.

Yet they speak of yearnings for your heart.

Yet they speak of yearnings for your love.

Look, if push comes to shove.

He turns away; don't look into his baby blues.

Look, if push comes to shove.

Say you've seen far too much.

Say you've seen enough; honestly, far too much.

But what am I to do?

Really, what am I to do?

When he wears that mask, that cloak over his heart,

Look, if push comes to shove

Allow him just one more kiss.

One more day eternally reminisce.

Like a fog light shining ever so bright

Oh, how expediently he lets go.

When I'm just about to internally, ignite

Melt through his gloved fingers like warmed snow.

When Will You Breathe Me Back?

By Mark Andrew Heathcote

When will you breathe me back from the dead?

When will you meet me, my heart's true breath?

Because I feel like a cave of emptiness

Because I feel like a void of loneliness

As though I were a sea of cold insurrection

Carried on a soul with no earthly direction

When will you breathe me back from the dead?

When will you meet me, my heart's true breath?

O, daughter of the wind, sweet siren of the reef

Don't ever forsake me for this, my eternal grief

To this stale wall of desolation

To this empty shell of my heart's abnegation;

When will you breathe me back from the dead?

When will you meet me, my heart's true breath?

O, if I call you like the moon on the sea,

Won't you change your tide back to me?

O, won't you listen to the harp call of my heart?

And let its music cheer you in an ancient dark

When will you breathe me back from the dead?

When will you meet me, my heart's true breath?

Blessed Imelda Lambertini

By Mark Andrew Heathcote

Blessed Imelda is no more.

Her heart was twined—

like a sycamore seed

taken on the wind to our sweet Lord.

Blessed Imelda is no more

she is one, without a doubt, joined—

the Incorruptible Saints

Hers is a vocation unquestionable forever more.

Blessed Imelda is no more

She prayed to her beloved Jesus.

And was discovered by nuns returning,

still in prayer, bent like some whitish hellebore.

Blessed Imelda is no more.

She received her communion.

The Holy Eucharist a year early,

and later was found dead on the floor,

Blessed Imelda is no more.

Each denied request increased her love.

It was said she died of pure love and joy.

Glass-encased, never to age or mature.

I would Love You Even If Your Name Were

By Mark Andrew Heathcote

I would love you even if your name were Drusilla.

I would love you even if your name were Morticia.

I would love you even if your name were Bellatrix.

I would love you even if your name were Raven.

I would love your thick black hair.

I would love your fiery red nails.

I would love you for the way you bite my skin.

I would love you because you are everything to me.

I would love you even if your name were Belladonna.

I would love you even if your name were Delora.

I would love you even if your name were Lola.

I would love you even if your name were Naenia.

Because I want to die in your arms.

Funerals and mourning mean nothing to me.

I'm a slave; I am lost to Perdita.

And Solanine, she loves me.

And Trista likes to follow me wherever I am.

Oh, and how Valonia she does covert me.

And Carey cradles me in the dark.

And Adrienne mops my brow and lights an ancient spark in my heart.

I would love you even if your name were Raven.

I would love your thick black hair.

I would love your fiery red nails.

I would love you for the way you bite my skin.

I would love you because you are everything to me.

So Pale and Hurtfully Prissy

By Mark Andrew Heathcote

Why does she come shadow dancing up my spine?

Doesn't she realise I've served a necromancer's time?

Melancholy is a thistle, a rose garland in black holy

her love, a so-called red beating heart, a coulee,

a furnace, a kiln, a blue broach of cracked enamel:

Why doesn't she sliver like a feline fox, mindful?

Into that toothless-fearless smiling dead cemetery

who is she to be so pale and hurtfully prissy?

God only deny me the light to slay this shadow

the strength to live and breathe again tomorrow.

A Lover's Migration

By Mark Andrew Heathcote

My shoulders were blotting paper for her tears

Naively, I dealt with all her bad nightmares.

Every day, her sanity was shaken.

Her grip on reality wasn't reawaken

I was there attentively listening

And it was all just - so exhilarating:

I, being the thread that held two seams together.

She wanted us to marry; you know? - Whosoever?

But like birds in the sky, I can't stay settled

I yearn to fly and eventually be resettled.

When the sun shines no more when seams are torn

I want to stay but have to leave love forlorn.

Dark Mirrors

By Mark Andrew Heathcote

There's always smoke, tears, and dark mirrors.

When I can't reach you

And I end up feeling like road kills, not quite dead.

That's when I want to leave and bleed.

Bleed blood in silence, listening to every heartthrob.

Asking what makes you tick, have I missed a trick?

Am I wrong? Are you right? Why on earth?

Did we fight again last night?

Is everything a spiral spinning on an access

On its course, but battling re-entry

Will I burn up or realign with you?

And if I do, will you love me?

Like I do you.

CATHERINE A. MACKENZIE's writings are found in numerous print and online publications. She writes all genres but invariably veers toward the dark—so much so her late mother once asked, "Can't you write anything happy?" (She can!)
Cathy lives in Halifax, Nova Scotia, Canada.

Website: writingwicket.wordpress.com

Flown Away

By Catherine A. MacKenzie

Love has flown,

Blown away like a leaf

Or a stone thrown

Into an ocean of grief,

Nothing can add

To loneliness to come...

A Loaded Gun

By Catherine A. MacKenzie

My heart is beating, ready to explode my pent-up love for you,

The timer is ticking, the pendulum swinging, my love continues to grow,

Our wires are tuned while we fuse together, moulding two lives as one,

But you pulled the trigger, without a care, without telling me,

You loaded and aimed, you poised to shoot,

I watched in disbelief at the man I loved when he cocked his head and glared at me,

I sensed the pain before I saw it coming, before the bullet tore free to pierce my heart.

Words

By Catherine A. MacKenzie

If I had invisible ink

I'd write a letter to you—

No! A book instead

For a letter would not be

Paper enough for words

I yearn to say.

I'd write invisibly

'Cause you'd not want to read

What I scribble.

But it would be a balm

Upon my heart to rid myself

Of words buried inside.

Uprising

By Catherine A. MacKenzie

The steam, hot melding into cold,
Rises from the ground
In the early morn,
The rush like a swarm of bees,
Crushing, electric, buzzing
In the dampness, waiting...

By day
I linger and watch
And wonder,
Captured by the essence of you
While withering into a cacophony of nerves
Amid whispers from the trees.

The cold hard steel of your form
Descends upon me at night when
I envelop you with my veiled love,
And I hide behind mascaraed lashes
While fearing the hush of
Fallen angels below.

Buy Me a Coffin; Dig Me a Hole

By Catherine A. MacKenzie

Can't stand the pain, oh the pain,
Not to mention the stain upon my soul.

I view the coffin not yet built...
The reprieve from ails and woes.

Old age's a bitch
—The Witch—
The wicked woman flying high in the sky...

I swear The Witch throws bad vibes at me—
And us: the guilty, the innocent, the unsuspecting.

Despite that, I eye the unbuilt coffin: fibreglass, steel, wood,

Oh, so many woods: mahogany, pine, pressboard.

I don't care what covers me—the colour or form of shroud,

Cover me in "whatever,"

I'm dead, right?

Will I know?

I won't care (or will I?).

Might I come back to haunt you because you didn't bury me properly?

Can I do that if I don't believe in ghosts or supernaturals?

Please—

Whatever your beliefs: no cremation.

I'll have enough burning in forever Hell

Without ashes within days of my untimely earthly death,

But—

Who knows...

Might I be granted a reprieve from sins?

Note: I don't want anyone to mourn for me. I lived a life—a great one—and tho I wish I could've lived longer, life is what it is, right? Death is unthwartable. Except for God (if you believe) no one is greater. Death is the ultimate in whatever form Death is: He/She/They/Furry/whatevers. Death is always everywhere (here, there)—always alive: able, ready, willing to catch us before we fall.

SHARMON GAZAWAY is a Dwarf Stars Award finalist. Her work appears in *The Forge, The Best of MetaStellar, NewMyths.com,* and in anthologies from Ravens Quoth Press, Black Spot Books, and others. Sharmon writes from the Deep South of the US, next door to a cemetery haunted by the wild cries of pileated woodpeckers.

Instagram @sharmongazaway

A Bout of Horrible Sanity

By Sharmon Gazaway

A bereft tree leans

as if weighted by the mourning

of the raven on its branches

the red I took for blossoms

are leaves clutching

with bloody grip grasping grey hands

refuse to free the tree

of its nightmarish burden.

Mist rolls in blurred undulations

across precisely measured squares

of black-and-white marble

(strangeness in proportion)

cool to the touch of reaching black grass

breaching the boundaries of time

set by silent sands

as through a glass—

a murky milky light

bears the cake-scent of joy departed

and hovers over all

but it is not the moon

and the mist swallows it.

Virginia's Mirror

By Sharmon Gazaway

is but a cipher

a blank where she should have been

a chill silver swallowing

of youth, beauty, and love

capturing the depth of nothingness

in its glassy shallows.

She has slipped its bonds

(so into the trunk it must go

like an oblong box of similar wood)

she is not there.

I finger the ornately carved frame

and fancy it carries

remnants of her scent—a dusky

blend of powdery violets

and mellow ivory keys—

fancy her lilting whisper *"la mia vita*

è tua" haunts the breeze. I cannot

bear to touch the tenebrous

unfeeling glass

and long to shatter it

but it would only serve

to multiply in its jagged fractals

my grief, my grief, my grief.

Notes: Virginia Clemm Poe's mirror was found in Poe's trunk after his death.
"La mia vita è tua"—"my life is thine"—Virginia was fluent in Italian; the line
is lifted from her Valentine poem to Poe, 1846 (it was written in English
originally). She died a year later.

JAMESON GREY Jameson Grey's work has been published in *Dark Recesses Press* magazine, *Dark Dispatch* and in anthologies such as *Chlorophobia: An Eco-Horror Anthology* from Ghost Orchid Press, *Let the Weirdness In: A Tribute to Kate Bush* from Heads Dance Press and *Penny Blood Tales* from Black Ink Fiction.

Website: jameson-grey.com

The Kiss of the House of Usher

By Jameson Grey

I lie here awake and reminisce

Something troubles me—a kiss…

In spring, they came to visit me,

My future brother, my bride-to-be,

Though the latter I did not know

'Til upon my doorstep first April, she did show.

He I'd known long, our kinship built strong

By years spent in study as Hippocrates' sons.

Of men and his brethren,

Of mothers of men, and sistren in kind,

I thought I knew the body well.

If only I'd known the mind.

Of the sister, I'd learnt naught.

In mystery to me, her life had been led.

Except perhaps had she taught?

A governess at one time she had been, Roderick said.

Dazzling she was—a perfect delight.

I thought we'd shared souls that fool's spring night.

We spoke discreetly of love,

As Roderick sat aside

Smiling, offering little above

"How it was meant to be!"—his beloved sister and me.

'Though a cousin to Roderick was Madeline, in truth,

Orphaned at birth, she came to his line.

Born the same day, the last of the Ushers,

So close did they grow—like twins, entwined.

Summer came and plans were laid.

Marriage to Madeline—

I, no longer a bachelor,

She, no longer a maid.

And I dismissed it as idle

When news came from friends

Who said, long beyond youth,

They were seen holding hands.

For they were something more than twins; I was warned

Even as Roderick led congratulations on honeymoon's dawn.

'Though in my wedded bliss,

I saw only a siblings' sweet kiss.

No longer pure Madeline,

Now Mrs P—— she was,

And thus, ended summer

Happily wed, the two of us.

As we ushered in the fall, a visit from the brother
With news he must leave.
"A position abroad," said he,
"But no need to grieve."

A tonic he produced to soften the blow
Glasses poured, the wine overflowed,
Roderick abstained—"My journey…" he claimed.
How fortunate, it seemed, o'er me, faintness came!

I felt myself fall into the ink—
The inky blackness of death…

When I awoke,
"Maddie," I croaked. "Where am I?"
Maddie's eyes wide in alarm,
"Look, he's alive! Alive," she cried.

But yet, in her voice, I detected no joy.
Roderick appeared—and revealed their ploy.
The wine held a potion—paralysis was full!
How I yet spoke was some miracle.

Still, Roderick thought it many days
Before I could regain
Any movement at all,
Any freedom from restraint.

He took Maddie's hand and leaned over the casket
Their lips joined, off slipped their masks
At once, where I had thought rumour amiss,
I saw it all now in that unnatural kiss.

The scraping of stone as they shut out the light
A glimpse of strained faces I took into that night.

The sarcophagus closed,
In my own cellar, cast,
Sealed in, immobile,
How long might I last?

Darkness oppressive,
Stale, dusty air.
I lay and I wondered
Who else would know where?

And for how long did I lie?

Minutes, days, hours?

Yet at last, I felt strength,

Slender hope flowers.

My fingertips ring with the tingle of life

My toes, they are wriggling

My eyes retain light

My breathing, though, strangles.

The long winter beckons,

I must resist the undiscovered land,

I scratch at the stone,

I must raise my hand.

Will shallow air sustain?

Will I scrape free?

I hear mirth from above.

Twin laughter at me?

My hand on the stone,

Pressed on the lid.

Alone, too weak to lift.

With two of them, it slid.

I'm trapped here, eternal

While they live above.

My house given over

To those I had loved.

Does anyone else suspect all that's remiss?

That my fate was once sealed—sealed, with that twins' kiss.

**First Published Love Letters to Poe,
Volume II: Houses of Usher,2022**

SHELDON WOODBURY has an MFA in Dramatic Writing from New York University. His short stories and poems have appeared in many horror anthologies. His poem, "The Midnight Circus", was an honourable mention for Best Horror 2017, and "The Madness of Monsters", is included in the 2021 HWA Poetry Showcase.

Forever

By Sheldon Woodbury

I'll slip like a whisper
through deathly veils
creeping through mire
with a haunting wail
you'll ask who I am
when I caress your throat
with skeletal hands of ashen smoke

We all pay a price
for our earthly sins
so there comes a time
when atonement begins
that's when I'll come
with a musty menace
a wispy phantom seething with vengeance

I'll savage your flesh
until nothing is left
except for your soul
that will never be blessed
I'll ravage that too
with a ravenous hunger
dragging you down to my deathly slumber

You said you only hurt
the ones you love
when we were married
in the realm above
where you murdered me
in a monstrous rage
trapping me in this rotted cage

But all that doesn't
matter anymore
because you're still the one
I hunger for
so now we'll be together
in this prison forever
your crumbling corpse and your ghostly lover

BARBARA SMITH published her debut children's picture book, *Otis Paul & Harry the Hairy Echidna,* in 2019. Her poetry is published in the *Zodiac* series, Australian Speculative Fiction, Deadset Press, Rosey Ravelston, *dyst Journal*, Specul8 Publishing and Ravens Quoth Press. Follow her on Twitter @BarbAnn, and on her website.

Website: lifeandbeyondblog.wordpress.com

THE RAVENS QUOTH PRESS

Forevermore

By Barbara Smith

The breath of the sea

brought you to the lap of my shore

bringing with it the temptation of

 Forevermore

You lingered until the gravity of your world

drew you back

whilst the echoes of your embrace

on the sandy shore sing

 Forevermore

TREVOR WRIGHT is a writer based in Peru, IL. His poetry explores life's intricacies, drawing inspiration from personal experiences. He lives with his wife and two daughters, whose presence deeply enriches his creative journey. Through his work, he reflects on both the ordinary and the extraordinary aspects of life.

Instagram: @wrightspoetry

Phantoms of Despair

By Trevor Wright

In the twilight of despair,

where shadows whisper secrets,

a lonely figure wanders through

the haunted corridors of memory.

Gloom shrouds the ancient manor,

its halls echoing with ghostly sighs—

footsteps of the past

trailing through the dust of forgotten years.

A raven perches on the window ledge,

its eyes gleaming with dark intent,

a silent sentinel

watching over the unravelling night.

Moonlight spills through cracked panes,

painting eerie patterns on the floor,

a spectral dance of light and dark,

where phantoms tread on unseen paths.

Whispers of lost love linger,

clinging to the cold, damp air,

each sigh a testament

to hearts broken and dreams undone.

Through the labyrinth of sorrow,

memories weave their mournful tales,

a tapestry of despair and longing—

threads of life frayed and torn.

In the distance, a tolling bell,

its mournful chime a dirge,

calling the weary soul

to rest in the embrace of eternal night.

For in the realm of shadows,

where Poe's spirit dwells,

every whisper is a story,

every shadow hides a secret,

and every heartache

sings a melancholy song of the soul.

TONIA KALOURIA, retired teacher and soap actress, pens her poems from quaint Chagrin Falls, Ohio, USA.

Two other Poe-esque poems appear in *Quoth the Raven*, and *A Glass of Wine With Edgar* anthologies. She has several humorous works at *littleoldladycomedy.com*, "Lighten Up!," and, "Take5ive," among others.

Twitter/X: @kalouriatvs

Ravin' Mad: Bugs are for the Birds!

By Tonia Kalouria

Once upon a Tuesday dreary,

as I scanned my email, weary,

I came upon a click-bait ad

that challenged all control I had.

"Try our '*delicious Bugs*,'" it said.

That idea, nothing more.

"You'll love our 'Cricket Crunch,'" it lied,

a theory quickly I denied,

but when they hawked their "Bugs Stir-fry":

I shrieked out loud, "I'd rather die!"

My psyche could bear no more.

Next up, they squawked: "Maggots in Brine":

"No, thank you, kids: Not *this* lifetime!"

"Sample our frozen 'Mealworms Meal:'"

My tummy's vote? No peck-appeal!

I screeched, "Never! Evermore."

But: "For *dessert*, a Locust Pie?!"

Taken aback, I could but cry:

"You're killing me; stop being wry!"

I threw the mouse down—had to fly—

The stomach screamed: "NO MORE!"

THOMAS R. KEITH resides in Austin, TX. His interests include horror fiction, the Gothic, and the history of lyric poetry. His work has appeared in several literary journals and anthologies.

Substack: thomasrkeith.substack.com

The Last Meeting

By Thomas R. Keith

On a grey and troubled evening,

As the mists blew from the sea,

All alone and all forsaken,

I bade Mary come to me.

"Do not leave me here to suffer,

Wrapped within my shroud of grief:

Mary, you who loved me truly,

Bring my anguished soul relief!"

Footfalls echoed through the hallways,

On the rough stones of the floor,

Light and gentle as a dancer:

Hark! A knock upon the door!

Quick I rose and threw it open,

Fearful lest the sound should fade:

There she stood, my precious Mary—

Nothing but a pallid shade.

As in swamplands, in the gloaming,

Wisps of light will slowly rise,

Play about the air, then vanish,

So was Mary to my eyes.

Gone her summer-sweet complexion,

Gone her cheeks' enthralling glow—

Paler now than when we laid her

In the tomb, a year ago.

"Oh!" I cried. "My lovely Mary,

True in death, as once in life,

How the cruel Fates betrayed us!

You who should have been my wife,

Come and feel my fervent kisses!

Come into my warm embrace!"

I reached for her, but softly moaning,

She turned aside her ghostly face

And spoke: "No man of flesh could hold me,

I am made of smoke and air.

Go, beloved, and forget me.

Woo another, young and fair.

She will share your warm embraces,

She will share your board and bed.

For your place is with the living,

Mine is with the silent dead."

Then the distant church bell, tolling,

Warned men of the midnight hour.

Mary gave a sigh and vanished,

Swifter than a wilting flower.

I will not heed my Mary's warning,

Will not take another bride.

When I hold my lonely wedding,

It will be at Mary's side.

There will be no cheers, no singing,

Nothing but a pall of gloom:

Our clergyman, the hooded Reaper,

Our bed, the dank and cobwebbed tomb.

DAWN DEBRAAL lives in rural Wisconsin with her husband, Red, a dorky dog, and a stray cat. She has published over 700 stories, poems, and drabbles. She co-wrote a novel, *what the hell happened to joan?* under the pen name of Garrison McKnight.

Website: linktr.ee/dawndebraal

My Dearly Departed

by Dawn DeBraal

A murder of crows in the old dead tree.

Be still my heart, are they here for me?

Close the windows, slam the door.

I cannot hear them anymore.

Their piercing cries say, "Blood will spill."

They'll have to take me against my will

My days are numbered, there's no reprieve,

There's not much time before I leave.

Then I awoke this morn in bed.

Who's been taken in my stead?

The crows are gone, but so is she.

My darling daughter, Emily.

I scream and cry, "Please bring her back.

Take me now, oh heart attack.

Drown me in the raging sea,

Only set my daughter free."

The Birds call back with raucous laughter

Leave me here, ever after

Alone I'll live for eternity,

without my darling Emily.

ERIC SHELMAN was born on Halloween, in Texas. He's a diverse poet who began writing shortly after reading Edgar Allan Poe's *The Raven*, which inspired him to be a poet, forever. He writes all sorts of poetic forms, including a few he has created and merged together.

Night-Mares

By Eric Shelman

After lying down to sleep

trying to obtain some much-deserved rest

waiting, wanting and hoping quick-fast deep asleep

unfortunately, and surprisingly, instead

Mare, came to visit, sitting on my chest

    suffocating me with his pulsating

        fearful, terrific, horrific, anxious, and hellacious

worlds and scenarios' sensations

Evermore, evilly energetically ecstatic

Forevermore, ferociously facetious

Nevermore, ceasing, appeasing, releasing

Cursed me like Poe's obsessive love for Lenore

bored boors doing core chores

more gory, lore crematory, yore damnatory

Tore me apart

bashed me on and through bloody vaulted

doors, floors, drawers

ghastly, vastly, lastly, and steadfastly

pouring pores, spores into my poorly wilted warrings

Soaring shrieking roars

sworn sleepless snores

ensnaring, scaring, daring, tarring stories

Carrying, tarrying and parrying me

as its rag doll

Caved, depraved, graved gave enslaved

as its afterlives diabolical, symbolical, parabolical,

and apostolical, glimpses.

ANTHONY PERCONTI lives and works in the hinterlands of New Jersey with his wife and kids. He enjoys well-crafted and engaging stories from across a variety of genres and mediums.

The Ages of the Bells: An Oracle

By Anthony Perconti

The lamp is lit, a dram is poured,

The man sits down to tell,

On this wild and windswept night,

Of the Ages of the Bells.

I. The Age of Silver

Bells of silver sing,

In Runic rhymes, making time,

The cold stars look down.

II. The Age of Gold

Golden bells ringing,

On the day of our union,

Hearts bursting with love.

III. The Age of Brass

Brazen bells scream out,

Shrieking out tales of terror,

Filling the night air.

IV. The Age of Iron

Iron bells tolling,

A ballad of total war,

The Ghoulish King laughs.

The verse complete, he quaffs his drink,

And replaces the ink-stained quill,

The man reviews his handiwork,

And shudders with a demonic thrill.

What dark muse sparked his soul,

To pen this carillon rhyme,

Oracular visions are transmitted,

A dire portend grips his mind.

Hear the tolling of the bells—Funerary bells!

The poet is overcome with dread,

Silent tears stream down his face,

For soon he would be dead.

In Tormentum Aeternum Requiescat!

By Anthony Perconti

Here I sit, awaiting my doom.

Twelve honest men have sealed my fate,

An appointment with the gallows, to swing until death.

Of nervous disposition, true! This I do freely admit,

But never one to be called mad, not I.

I took great pains. I was oh so cautious, oh so cunning.

A point of pride-I did my work and did it well. Heh.

Those constables had no inkling,

Of what lay secreted beneath their feet.

Search and question, to your contentment,

That room, its secrets would it keep. Yet—

A fly in the ointment, a fissure in the vase,

A crack in the foundation, a deformity in the blade.

That heart—HIS blasted heart will NOT stop beating!

Its ghostly echo haunts me still.

Like a glove that knows its hand.

In slumber there is neither solace nor respite.

His Pale Blue Eye peers down from shivered skies.

That monstrous turquoise orb, that damned spot is All Seeing,

The Glare of Judgment—I cannot hide.

My chamber door creaks open, a lambent shaft pierces within,

The guards will escort me to the gibbet,

I rise up to meet my fate. When—

That hideous heart, that hellish tattoo ceases!

Astounded by the silence, tears of joy begin to well,

All for naught-my hopes are shattered!

I fall further down the spiral—I exchange one horror for another,

An eidolon attends me in the cell.

That dear old man, that kin to vultures,

Materialises before my very being.

There he stands, Death's Black Shadow,

Terrible smile devoid of warmth or pity.

Those eyes bore into my very soul,

One bloodshot, the other glaucus.

A susurration in my ear;

"My dear boy, how I've missed you so."

Terror overtakes my senses,

I let forth with a scream!

The guards rush in, they pass right through him!

His smile grows wider-the Beckoning Void.

I stand upon the scaffold, hands bound at my back,

That dear old man, a bloody shambles, whispers;

"We have eternity to become reacquainted."

The trap drops open; the world goes black.

In tormentum aeternum requiescat!

KERRI MERRIAM-BUCKTON is a Canadian author of several genres. She has been published with Dark Rose Press, Sweety Cat Press, and has published her first novel, *Where the Trees Know You*. When she is not writing, she devotes most of her time to her husband and three children.

Website: kerrimbuckton.com

Sanctuary Park

By Kerri Merriam-Buckton

Oft forgotten and alone

Midst tombstones loneliness thrives

With only dashes cut in stone

To show start and end of lives.

Whispered voices in the wind

Like tides, rise and fall

The afterlife now begins

They answer heaven or hell's call.

On their resting place I tread

Souls locked inside death's cage

I say a prayer for the dead

That they find rest and quell their rage.

How long have I been afraid of death

Dreaded every minute's pass

And its cold fingers on my neck

Yet now find peace upon this path.

Giving my respect

To whom before me came

I make my solitary trek

To the stone that bears my name.

I lie atop the greenest hill

In this place called Sanctuary Park

I no longer feel the chill

And surrender to the dark.

Hold Your Breath

By Kerri Merriam-Buckton

I hold it in as I walk by

For fear the dead will hear and try

To steal my life from inside me

Snatch the very breath I breathe.

Behind wrought iron gates

Silence is deceiving, they lie in wait

Supposedly sleeping, resting in peace

But they're really waiting on souls to feast.

Lost spirits deeply scorned

The crow cries out, so you are warned

Hold it in, hold your breath

So you may not yet be claimed by death.

First Published October 2021

SARAH DAS GUPTA is an 82-year-old writer who has lived and taught English in UK, India and Tanzania. She started writing after an accident which left her unable to walk without the aid of crutches. Writing has been a great help in providing an inspiration and a challenge. Her work has been published in over 150 magazines and anthologies.

The Stolen Heart

By Sarah Das Gupta

Into the forest, dark, fearful,

I ventured, looking for my love.

Branches of the shady pine trees

stretched strong arms to stop my search.

On a tall, majestic oak tree,

perched a raven black as the night,

its wings outstretched regal, kingly,

sweeping, silent, ahead of me.

As I followed the moonlit pathway,

glimpses of blue silk between the trees

left me hoping to find my lost dear.

The gloating bird flew ahead of me.

The raven perched on a black crag;

in dread fright, I saw the fearful sight.

My love lay cold in the pale moonlight;

what could I do to aid her dire plight?

Her hair hung golden in the silver light,

her eyes stared, frozen as she lay.

I saw only a bloodstained cavity, no heart!

Such depravity to peck her heart away.

REBECCA KOLODZIEJ grew up in South Wales, UK. She has always been a fan of writing, particularly horror.

Her debut poetry collection is a letter to the darkest parts of her mind, and her first personal dark poetry project.

Follow her poetry blog on Facebook for updates and new material on upcoming projects.

Facebook: @Heartless-Whispers-112886421692523

The Spiral of Madness

By Rebecca Kolodziej

The spiral of madness

Is a malicious thing

It caws in the dark—

A shadowy thing—

A reflection of a fever dream

Is it there or is it not?

A melancholy ghost

Of what time has not forgot

When the dark swallows

A brittle mind

It is a treacherous thing

A malignant cancer like the

Beating of black wing

Obsidian plumage carpets the floor

In the crack of the window

Something pipes, "Nevermore"

In the pale face of the moonlight

A glossy black eye blinks

"It is naught but my mind,"

She begins to think

But again, comes the cry

Of this Harbinger of Death

A symphony of anguish

Stretched out on its breath

Mercy black vanishes like

The wind

Flutter byes, crooning lullabies—

Lost amidst overwrought dreams

She lies in her bed—

Dreaming awake

A shadow grows, uncanny moans

Bedevilled by the dead

Madness screeches

And she beseeches to stare at cold

Stone wall

A flutter and a rustle, and a shadow

stands tall

roosting at the end of her bed—

Eyes once black now blazing red

"'Tis naught but by mind, some foul

Vision it has conjured "

With heart hammering in her chest

She began to wonder

Was her mind sickly?

"'Tis not,"

the stoic statue said

And then It skipped and hopped

and her heart

Almost popped when it reached

near her head

"Beast be gone, leave thy alone.

I am sick and you are just a dream."

But when the shadow mass, uttered

"Alas,

I am here to feast upon the dead."

And now afright, her pallor white

She stared into that glossy eye

"I am not dead."

"Lies," it said and it soon

began to croak

And as life left her turning cold

she began to choke

"Thing of evil, you take what not is yours."

Through a cackle and a murmur, it rasps

"Your soul, Evermore"

OLIVIA ARIETI 's poems appeared in *Women In Judaism, The Wanderlust Review, VWA: Poems For Haiti, Cliterature, The Harsh And The Heart, Pagan Friends, The Expeditioner's Guide To The World, Bridging the Cultural Divide Anthology, Feile-Festa, Haiku Of The Dead, Obama-Mentum Anthology, The Seasons, Trouvaille Review, Poetica* Clarendon House Books.

Once Upon a Rapture

By Olivia Arieti

Once upon a kingdom

By the sea,

No love equalled ours

And we let its fire

Wantonly burn

Youth and body

In rabid embraces

Till the angels,

Wicked fairies,

And my kinsmen,

Heinous monsters,

Envied its beauty

And sent a gelid,

Killer wind

To punish my soul.

Now from my abysmal

Sepulchre,

Forever without you,

I hear you crying

To the moon,

To the stars,

And tell about

Your consuming

Pain

As the pitiless

Tides

Thrust back

Your tears

And mock

The illusion

Of eternal

Love.

Dreary Midnights

By Olivia Arieti

"Nevermore", she cried

From the deadly abode

Where beauty fades

And yields to darkness.

And now no raven

Tapping

At my chamber door,

No demons, angels

From the land of yore,

Will bring me back

My sweet Lenore,

My ethereal maiden,

The delirious dream

That lifts my soul

And lets it fall

Upon the folly

Of my midnights

Dreary.

The Final Toll

By Olivia Arieti

The bells were tolling

The final knell

The mournful knell

The bells,

The hell awaiting

Already feasting,

The night was shrieking

The Dead were creeping

Wakened

By the tolling,

By the pealing

Of the bells

And all at once

Undead,

Snaked out

To listen

To the dooming

To the blasting

Everlasting

Of the bells

With hearts

Still singing,

They flock and float,

Stream and storm

To the steeple

Just to warn

Of the horrors,

Of the terrors,

Of the loss

Of mortal glory

When chimes

Turn into

Knells

With no more

Tinkling,

No more

Jingling

No more swelling

With delight

In the no more

Balmy night

Till the tolling,

Till the knelling

Forever silence…

And the Undead

Hear no more.

NAOMI PLISKOW has been writing poetry since childhood, but only recently has begun to share it with others. Several of her poems are scheduled to appear in upcoming editions of various literary magazines. Her agented nonfiction book, *Ungrowth*, has yet to be published. She lives outside Philadelphia

The Glutton

By Naomi Pliskow

with apologies to, and with the greatest admiration for, E. A. Poe

Once upon a midnight scary, while I languished, buzzed, and very

Hungry, thumbing through the various offerings of an online store—

While I nodded, nearly napping, suddenly there came a tapping,

As of someone gently rapping, rapping at my mancave door.

"It's delivery," I muttered, "tapping at my mancave door—

Likely this and nothing more."

Ah, distinctly I recall that it was in the early fall;

And I had given it my all to keep my marriage from Death's door.

Bummed, I faced the next tomorrow—vainly I had sought to borrow

From my phone escape from sorrow—sorrow for my lost Lenore—

For the sweet and lovely woman whom her parents named Lenore—

Nameless here for evermore.

And the joyful recognition of each gilded acquisition

Thrilled me–as I sent each thing I wanted cart-bound, wanting more;

So that now, to calm the beating of my heart, I stood repeating

"'Tis the GrubHub guy entreating entrance at my mancave door—

Bearer of my dinner seeking welcomed entrance at my door;—

                                    This it is and nothing more."

Presently the urge grew stronger; hesitating then no longer,

"Dude," I said, "I'm very sorry, your forgiveness I implore;

But the fact is I was scrolling, and so gently you came rolling,

And so faintly you came tapping, tapping at my chamber door,

That I scarce was sure I heard you"—here I opened wide the door—

                                    Darkness there and nothing more.

Deep into that darkness peering, long I stood there wondering, sneering,

Doubting, dreaming dreams no sober person likely dreamt before;

But the silence was unbroken, and the stillness gave no token,

And the only word there spoken was the whispered word, "Lenore?"

This I whispered, and an echo murmured back the word, "Lenore!"—

                                    Merely this and nothing more.

Back into my mancave turning, four chugged beers within me churning,

Soon again I heard a tapping slightly louder than before.

"Crap," I said, "there's something still that's lurking on my window sill;

I'll go find out what is the drill, this weird occurrence I'll explore—

I'll let my heartbeat chill a second and this mystery explore—

'Tis the wind and nothing more!"

Open here I flung the shutter, when, with many a flit and flutter,

In there stepped a big black bird, a kind I'd never seen before;

Hopped right in and dropped a feather; never asking why or whether;

Flew, and passing up my leather chair, perched near my mancave door—

Perched upon my great big flatscreen sitting near my mancave door—

Perched, and sat, and nothing more.

So then, I with bird beguiling, took a selfie, broadly smiling,

While it groomed its wings and fluffed up inky feathers that it wore,

"I will put this out on TikTok," I said, "with words that you did knock

Upon my door, escaped from your flock, like no one has seen before—

Dude, what should I even call you, perching near my mancave door?"

Quoth the Raven, "Never More."

I was dumbstruck by the bird who, yes; it seemed had really heard

My question, though its answer was a thought that I deplore;

For whosoever can stop wanting all the stuff the world is flaunting

Getting no more would be daunting: I must always have some more—

Particularly while I suffer, missing newly gone Lenore,

> Horror: saying, "Never More."

But the raven, sitting lonely near my exit, uttered only

Those two words, that horrid threat denying succour, what a bore!

Nothing further then he uttered—not a feather, then he fluttered—

When I stumbled, landing on my butt, heard nothing from that shore—

Then I asked that, come tomorrow, if he would go out my door.

> And the bird said, "Nevermore."

Startled by this word emitted by the frightful bird who flitted,

Now between my drum set and my many crumpled cans galore,

Some unglued dude must have taught him wretched words, and then I caught him

With words fraught, him lurking, here, around my dim, dank mancave door—

With the dark and hopeless name that made me shiver to my core

> Clearly stated: "Nevermore."

But the raven had me puzzled, so I popped a top and guzzled,

Wondering what "more" he had thought of when he uttered "never more;"

Not a clue what he was after. Tripping on my Stratocaster

Thinking sadly of my past, Her, stubbed-toe-hobbled to my door

Wondering grimly what this avian thing might know about Lenore—

What this gruesome bird, repeating just the word that I abhor

Meant in croaking, "Nevermore."

This I sat engaged in guessing, but no questions, then expressing

To the bird whose eyes burned straight into my not-yet-chiselled core;

This and more I sat divining, with my head, now limp, reclining

On pool table's bright green lining, pizza boxes scattered o'er,

On whose bright green felted lining, or beneath it, on the floor,

She shall lie, ah, nevermore!

Then, a formless thought arrived, that, just perhaps, Lenore contrived

To send this beast to perch on flatscreen sitting near my mancave door.

"So dude," I cried, "if Lenore sent you, tell her that I don't repent. You

Tell her that that non-event should not have sent her out the door—

And that biker babe was nothing, she was just a lucky score."

Quoth the Raven, "Nevermore."

"Jerkoff!" said I, butt-faced scum! Just perched there, with your plumy bum—

Go tell her she was a complainer, standing at my mancave door,

Posed with hands upon her hips, and launching falsehoods from her lips,

She counted out my faults and slips, the self-absorption at my core—

I know she'll say she's sorry and come slinking through my chamber door."

Quoth the Raven "Nevermore."

"Fine!" I yelled. "I've had enough, then. You and I are, finally, both Men—

There are many more hot women out beyond my mancave door!

Swiping right will be my thing, man, and at clubs you'll be my wingman!

I'll forget her leaving's sting, man, and I'll order stuff that's More!

Lots of women draped between the stuff I'll order from the store!"

Quoth the Raven "Nevermore."

"Bastard!" I cried, that makes no sense, I owe her no recompense,

So why should I be punished, when it was my fragile heart she tore.

In the end, I just was outbid— there was nothing wrong that I did;

So, I'll have no more of Cupid, since my dentist took Lenore—

That rare and radiant maiden, that disgusting bitch Lenore.

Said I, snarling, "Nevermore!"

Then I really came to hate him, and I started to berate him,

But, still hungry, I just ate him. He was stringy to the core

And of course, a bit like chicken, though his liver made me sicken,

But with no regret was stricken, as I evened up the score—

And I belched with glee in thinking I had evened up the score.

Said I, drooling, "Nevermore!"

So now a raven, never flitting, is not talking here, nor sitting

On my glorious gleaming flatscreen just next to my mancave door;

Not a judgment does he utter, not a twitch, a word, a flutter,

None about that rotten slut, her pulsing absence, my Lenore;

All alone I'll bear that absence of my bitch from Hell, Lenore.

Said no raven "Nevermore."

There is no shadow, shame, or sorrow, just what I can get tomorrow—

His opinion I'll not borrow, as I shout out "Ever More!"

LINDAANN LOSCHIAVO is a native New Yorker, Elgin
Award winner, and member of British Fantasy Society, HWA, SFPA,
and The Dramatists Guild.

Current books: *Messengers of the Macabre, Vampire Ventures,
Apprenticed to the Night* (UniVerse Press, 2024), and *Always Haunted:
Hallowe'en Poems* (Wild Ink, October 2024).

Twitter/X: @Mae_Westside

Poe and His Women

By LindaAnn LoSchiavo

Ligeia, Annabel Lee, and Berenice,

Supernal beauties, pleasing to the eye,

Were temporary mates and marble-cheeked

Like timeless funerary monuments.

Tremaine's Rowena, Lady Madeline,

Insidiously felled and pushed offstage,

Had met goth's Mister Goodbar on the page.

First, females got top billed — — then burying.

What makes an author kill his heroines?

Recognising a woman's grave could be

His open throat, death-bed vows memorised,

Poe's pen despaired of daylight's finitude.

Clocks ticking, wasted time, reminded him

The coffin waits and pages lie half done

In desolation. Anonymity's

Curse frightens writers more than Roderick

Encountering his sister's open crypt.

Unholy was the hesitation left behind,

His desk in disarray, the inkwell filled,

Quills conjured up another sinister

Enchantress. Edgar's poised to start again.

Lady Madeline Usher's Revenge

By LindaAnn LoSchiavo

"We have put her living in the tomb!"
–Poe, The Fall of the House of Usher, 1839

Poe's story didn't cover Roderick

With glory, shoving me inside that crypt

Alive though bored to death—shut up, my sole

Companion him, doomed gloomy twin. How droll

To dream he'd benefit—sole ownership—

As if our home, with that décor, was hip,

Dark passages, frayed, sombre tapestries,

Tarnished armorial mementoes. He's

A hoarder. Junk became his "rare antiques."

Insipid arguments were his technique

For keeping me unmarried and distressed

About his health, discouraging my guests,

Manipulative, daring suicide

Each time I saddled up my horse. A bride

I might have been, a beauty in my youth.

Rod got what he deserved and that's the truth.

Annabel Lee Breaks Her Silence by the Sea

By LindaAnn LoSchiavo

— *Inspired by "Annabel Lee," the last complete poem written by Edgar Allan Poe*

It was too many years ago that he,

Dishonourably discharged, introduced

Himself to me. I ran a B and B

Then: "Kingdom by the Sea" in Miami.

He claimed he'd keep me from the "Tyranny

Of Ordinary." I replied, "Can you

Clean drains, fix pipes with a mortician's care?"

"Winged seraphs," he sighed, adding, "Sounds dreamy."

He wasn't in touch with reality,

Kept telling guests I owned a *sepulchre.*

Since this is Florida, the reference

Eluded tourists. *Still.* It rankled me.

His nihilism had reached the enth degree.

Folks want to tan here, not defenestrate.

A swell mechanic, sure, but his morose

Mindset was only fit for poetry.

Then hurricanes uprooted my palm trees,

Chilling and killing income by the sea,

Chilling and killing my prized B and B.

While sweeping up debris, we disagreed.

Storm winds swept me into the sounding sea.

How strange. He calls me *bride*, sees my *bright eyes*,

Mourns by my sepulchre built near the sea.

Famous, he's published now by FSG.

NICK ROMEO, when not at his nine-to-five occupation which is strongly situated in the STEM fields, he engages in various creative outlets such as 3D digital renderings, electronic music, writing, sewing, and photography. Nick presently lives in Pittsburgh with his wife and two cat-children: Megatron and Tempest.

Dear Raven

By Nick Romeo

Dear Raven,

Maybe you're an angel who hit a low branch or ignored the directions back to your realm, causing your wings to fall off. Since that time, you have been painting over your white robes with black matte, taking on the mantle of a bird of prey. You pick at my decaying brain, sipping the infection out through my ears, all while whispering for me to remain strong and resist the gloom. You have helped me to remove that vile carrion from my psyche, scratching and digging with sharpened talons deep into my marrow. I have come to understand your true objectives, not as a portent of the apocalypse, but as a guardian. I can see that enlivening glow from your core shining through your eyes—that area you could not cover.

MAX BINDI is an Italian multimedia artist and poet. His work has appeared in several Literary Magazines including: *The Horror Zine, Aphelion, The Sirens Call eZine, Lovecraftiana* and elsewhere, as well as in a variety of notable Poetry Anthologies by SFPA, Hellbound Books, The Ravens Quoth Press and many more.

Deadly Song

By Max Bindi

You know the light bends

pain goes straight to the point

the blackest sea and the darkest sky blends

till you can hardly see their joint.

You know time is nothing

but an eerie transitional toy

It will bury all things

that we cannot destroy

Now lie beside me in this unearthly dream

Now lie beside me in this haunted room

Now lie beside me endlessly

between the dingy glitter

and the dazzling gloom

and kiss me deadly

one more time.

You know there's nobody in the crowd

one too many phantoms in our solitude

the winds murmur our names aloud

when alien shadows roam in the wood

and there are no more comforting hollow words

only your stone-cold black lips

strange memories sliding forward

with no ominous time left to keep

Now lie beside me in this unearthly dream

Now lie beside me in this haunted room

Now lie beside me endlessly

between the dingy glitter

and the dazzling gloom

and kiss me deadly

one more time.

**First published Sirens Call Ezine,
Dec 2022**

MARION COSEY is originally from Yellow Springs and is a law student at the University of Pennsylvania Carey Law School. Inspired by Edgar Allan Poe, he advocates for the continuation of traditional poetry. Beyond writing, Marion enjoys outdoor walks and music of all kinds, finding inspiration and relaxation in nature and melodies.

LinkedIn: linkedin.com/in/marion-cosey-22a76742

The Serpent

By Marion Cosey

Late upon an autumn bitter, as the stars arrayed their glitter,

When Polaris was the most enchanting of the eve's decor,

Sat I at my window squarely, seeing only just and barely

By the glowing stars that sparely lit the tarnish of my floor,

And the starlit clouds of dust that hovered near the tarnished floor—

> Just by these and nothing more.

Just outside my window shutter, I espied a raven flutter—

Pecking at the glass and casting wretched shadows on the floor;

"There is no one to awaken in this place—" I moaned unshaken,

As I languished there forsaken by the treacherous Lenore—

By the warped and wicked traitor who the demons named Lenore—

> Who would wrong me—nevermore!

When the bird resumed its wander, there ablaze and gleaming yonder,

Sat the pole star, only this time shining brighter than before;

From my window I sat thinking "'Tis to me that she is winking!"—

Ever and anon while swilling spirits stilled from Lethe's shore—

But alas, did drinking spirits that were stilled from Lethe's shore

Dull my heart, but nothing more.

Soon thereafter, I heard knocking that aroused me into walking

Hastily to greet the company that tarried at my door.

But the dark had not subsided, so that I was only guided

Slowly by the glow provided by the pole star on the floor—

Shining on the dusty glass and dimly shone upon the floor—

Solely this and nothing more.

There, within the unabating darkness, stood a woman waiting

From a house of ill repute—salacious in the garb she wore.

Said I there, "I must inquire, maiden, would thee fain retire?

Quell I must this vengeful fire stirring in my spirit's core!

For thy ember hair and emerald eyes shall soothe this spirit's core—

These alone and nothing more."

In a sombre room the lowly woman let her dress down slowly—

And for me to join her in disrobing, did she so implore.

She then freed her bosoms, tightly held beneath her gown and slightly

Grinned as it descended lightly to the tarnish of the floor—

And upon my bed she lay, abandoning the tarnished floor—

Just with flesh and nothing more.

Resting on a pillow, wedding nipple to the satin bedding

She revealed her back unto the heavens where the hallowed soar.

There, I saw a red ophidian fashioned down her back's meridian

And its eyes were bleak obsidian—blackness never seen before.

Thought I, "'Tis an odd thing I have surely never seen before—

Birthed from ink, but nothing more."

"Thou art but a lifeless feature—" I surmised then of the creature,

Whose uncanny visage was the fruit my drunken musing bore—

With my interest now invested and my vision uncontested,

My attention was arrested by the artistry this woman wore—

"What—" I thought, to call this carnal work of art this woman wore.

Hissed the serpent, "Evermore."

Heeding not my vague suspicion, given, per my intuition,

Never could a human bandy with a speaking carnivore;—

"Certainly, the serpent dreaded for deceiving mortals treaded

Only in the tales embedded in the tomes of holy lore—"

Thought I, "Still though—one will only find in works of gothic lore

Names that sound like 'Evermore.'"

Then the evening dark grew thicker, yet refulgent was the flicker

Of the stars within her lidless gaze— a glimpse I did adore—

And my nose was not eluded by the ambrette she exuded,

While she lie there still—denuded like a seashell washed ashore—

But relinquished, like a seashell that the tide would leave ashore

Would I linger evermore!

While our flesh was coalescing, tenderly was I caressing

Smooth unspoiled skin, and with my tongue from nave to neck I tore.

Though the serpent spoke obscurely, I knew it was red ink purely,

"Shortly to my senses surely—" I thought "I shall soon restore—"

And again, while I embraced her flesh, before they could restore—

Hissed the serpent, "Evermore."

In the sheets I deeply pondered how my bitter soul had wandered

From my home unto the sordid halls of Comus to explore.

Briefly, I took respite knowing after this ignoble going,

That these sheets in starlight glowing never forth would bear Lenore;—

Then the stranger uttered "Ah, was that her name?— 'Lenore?'"

"Silence!" Said I, "Nothing more!"

I ignored the riddle laden query from the naked maiden

Since I know the name "Lenore", I outwardly did not outpour—

Still, my ears had not been swindled, but the anger that had dwindled

Now was surely thus rekindled by this crimson carnivore—

For again I heard the Delphic stranger's crimson carnivore

Softly whisper "evermore."

Still did I suppose this creature nothing but a lifeless feature,

But my breast, now sore of wary caution, I could not ignore—

With my fervent zeal deflated and this undertaking hated,

I thought "Now that I am sated by this wench I do deplore,

What comeuppance shall I suffer for this mischief I deplore?"

Hissed the serpent, "Evermore."

"Duppy!—" I cried, "of damnation! Ancient token of temptation!

More incarnadine than any hate my heart hath known before!

Scarlet foe of my creator, does there wait perdition greater

Fitting for the fiendish traitor who the demons named Lenore?—

For the warped and wicked traitor who the demons named Lenore!"

                              Hissed the serpent, "Evermore."

"Duppy!—" I cried, "of damnation! Ancient token of temptation—

Yet hast thou set loose the fury tormenting my spirit's core!

Let wherever *she* may wallow dreadful trails of ruin follow—

May her spirit wander hollow till her mane is thronged with hoar—

Till her skin is stricken by the years that plague her locks with hoar!

                              Hissed the serpent "evermore."

Down I struck the stranger yelling, "Thou shall not forsake my dwelling—

Thee who secretly escaped the cherub guarded yards of yore—

May thy errand be completed lest my peace be further cheated

By the soul of who retreated to the night beyond my door!

Spare no punishment *Uhtceare* for that soul beyond my door!"

Hissed the serpent, "Evermore."

And I looked with rage undying thereupon the stranger crying

In the pale light from Polaris lingering upon the floor—

Then the stranger, ever shaking, stole into the starlight, breaking

Swiftly through the doorway taking too the creature that she bore—

But, throughout the empty halls, the anger that its hissing bore

Echoed there—forevermore!

LINDA MCCAULEY FREEMAN is the award-winning poet of *The Family Plot* (Backroom Window Press, 2022) and *The Marriage Manual* (BWPress, 2024). Lines from one of her poems are displayed at the Civil Rights Memorial Museum in Montgomery. She has an MFA from Bennington and was poet-in-residence, the Putnam Arts Council.

Website: LindaMcCauleyFreeman.com

Nevermore

By Linda McCauley Freeman

And Raven said, "Nevermore"

and swept her wings into a flutter-flight

leaving me thick with longing. Deep

against no darkness peering,

just that blazing orange searing,

rapping, tapping against my damned

heart's door. Only this, not more.

Doubting, dreaming, broken, bitten,

all within me burning, churning,

I sat alone where she had left,

imprint still on my sofa's lining,

leaving her shape and the echoing silence

of her departing. And I, seared

by her shadow, shall sing nevermore.

THE RAVENS QUOTH PRESS

SHIKHANDIN is the *nom de plume* of an Indian writer who writes for adults and children. Her published books include *After Grief* (Red River, India), *Impetuous Women* (Penguin RHI), *Vibhuti Cat* (Duckbill-Penguin RHI), *Immoderate Men* (Speaking Tiger, India). Her work has been widely anthologised, and published worldwide in journals.

Instagram: @writershikhandin

Bells

By Shikhandin

There were bells attached to his name.

One for each whim. She heard them chime

beneath her tongue every time

it ran over her bruises. She remembers

the wetness of the day. Staccato of rain

on asbestos. The salt of her wounds.

The tang of pain.

Chimes struck spells. Each bell pulled. Each string

made her do different things.

Her wounds etched maps, secret paths.

The rituals of his worship. Days rolled

like thunder. Time struck no notes.

Until the day she scattered

the bells. A cascade of charms

descending. And danced. How

she danced against the lime washed walls.

The puppet shows of her past. Mad

rain dance. Frenzied totem dance.

She was the marionette cut loose

now. The voodoo doll with its own

mind. Extended arms embracing

wild wind. Wild will. Love

was just blood flowing now.

Tooth for bloody tooth.

The Gypsy Woman
of the Cooum

By Shikhandin

Skin so slicked-down black
she could have sprung from the depths
of the *Cooum—that, what was
once river,
now uncoils like a snake grown sluggish
after gorging on the city's offal.

She walks the streets at dawn singing
her leaf rustling song. Her eyes inked out
from pots of dead night, blink
away invisible spider's webs, festooning
lampposts and trees.
Her moist medusa-head of hair hisses at the sun.

And there is a twist of indecipherable metal

at her ankle, the right one with the toes

splayed out as if to kiss the road. And then

there are her hips

grasping the freshly laid day.

They say that she is a thief

of many things. They say that the stick in her hand

has a magnetic head meant to lift clean

our magpie-collection of watches and baubles.

They say she takes babies from their cradles

and blows spells into them, so they turn out crooked

in their hearts or in their hands and legs.

When she stops to eat, her bellybutton opens

up like a carnivorous flower.

The nipples of her generous breasts peep

from her blouse like twin frogs in a dark well. And when

she is drunk, she lugs invisible totems after her.

She swings invisible amulets and charms.

When she mutters, her night eyes

take on the colours of a day broken

into a thousand histories. So, when she walks

by our street, the dogs are unsettled and shy.

The crows crouch and bob

their heads, beady eyes winking.

But the cats hold their tails high.

For once the cats walk free.

*The Cooum is a refuse choked river that flows through Chennai.

First published in *Cha: An Asian Literary Journal*,
April/May 2012

L.M. MAGGIO is an American writer and 18th-century fifer. She lives with her husband and completely reasonable number of cats, all crammed into a 19th-century abode. Ms Maggio, a librarian, has appeared in *Corvus Review, Defenestration* and *Little Old Lady Comedy* and more. Read more at her website.

Website: LauraMaggioWrites.com

Tribute

By L.M. Maggio

October settles desolate, amongst the dust and dread

The hoary moon, at her edges, blushing embered red

A slicing wind mercilessly rends my aching heart

And with her malic'd intent to shred all solace apart

Nyx commands the clouds in a sooty swarming swath

Blinding my dimm-ed sight on this curs-ed woodland path.

Closer, dear, yet ever closer do approacheth I;

I shall seeketh you in life, in death; on earth and heaven's sky

I shall uphold the oath unto the angels of which I duly swore

And never shall we part again; together evermore.

Treading soft upon the season's carpet of decay

I spy your silhouette in shadows, spirits of black and grey.

I approach your form as the moth is drawn to flame—a slave.

Bearing a love so wretched, as deep and mournful as the grave

Ancient terror—an emptiness—bloomed within me when you left

Growing darker, yawning, howling—leaving my soul bereft.

Gaping wider in that chasm moaned a ghastly wind

But now I yearn to drink your light once dearly held within

I tremble at your beauty, which tears chordae tendineae

Your countenance slightly angled, luminous—turned away

Awaiting me sorrowfully—as still as death, as stone

While I admire cheek and eyelash, slender build and fragile bone.

Closer, dear, yet ever closer do approacheth I;

We shall join in love anon with heaving breath and heavy sigh

This fervid union a bless-ed balm to my withered core

And never shall we part again; together evermore.

Can you sense my creeping shadow? Taste my deep despair?

But as an eidolin, stand ye trapped still'd in fraught nightmare.

O suddenly, I recall! I regret roaming upon this path

Stepping back, I shrink from phantoms of your hatred and your wrath

Borne from my past treachery, your demons howl in tortured prayer

I betrayed your trust, slain your love for but one brief affair.

And for these sins I'd bound my soul to realms of sulphurous hell

And pray in anguish'd tones for pardon, for your repulsion to dispel.

My mind—corrupted—entreateth me run from ruin, from fear

My heart, besieged with madness, obliges feet to step e're near.

Alas! I crave forgiveness— Save me from madness' cold grip!

Your stillness breaks—though head still bowed—a quirk lies upon your lip.

Ensnared by lips curl-ed in the shape of Cupid's bow

The veil you wear shrouds treasure, solely of which I know.

Though your silence is a phantom, in that smile I sense your pardon

Your mercy runneth through me—salvation!—here in death's still'd garden.

And with that blessing, silent, we may finally be united,

I step forward in this churchyard, O love! To be requited!

Closer, dear, yet ever closer do approacheth I;

In this city of the dead I walk—the moment nearly nigh

My guilt has been assuaged, heart burning with ardour

And never shall we part again; together evermore.

At last I reach your marker, caress polished marble fervently

Your likeness—your monument!—standing watch for all eternity

Grasping hand cold as porcelain, kissing lips as stiff as mortis

I withdraw my dirk, blade glinting, one slice for your forgiveness

With heavy sigh, I lay at sculpted feet of whom I adore

As my essence seeps on this hallowed ground;

We are together evermore.

KATYA HUZAU is a poet, born and raised in Philadelphia. Currently, she is a senior at Hamilton College, earning her BA in Creative Writing. When she isn't writing, she can be found baking, hanging out with friends, and spending time with her dog, Arthur.

Dear Poe

By Katya Huzau

Dear Poe,

Maybe instead of Annabel
    you could covet me,
I know you loved her long,
    your beautiful maiden Lee
but if you ever tire
    from the love you both shared, I'll be
in a field below wingèd seraphs,

    my body planted by a tree.
Having spent my days
    envying you and she,
I will be your light reversing her night,
    waking you from your dreams
    as you sleep there by the sea,
    next to her tomb by the sounding sea.

FRANCES JO KENNEDY GROSSMAN has three daughters, Amy, Holly, and Francey, who inspire her writing. With a Yankee father and Alabama mama, she grew up in Pennsylvania, and is a graduate of Emory University's Interdisciplinary Program. She loves the ocean and paints the sky.

Perhaps to Write

with Impunity

By Frances Jo Kennedy Grossman

My great imaginative inspirations diminish,

(those ecstatic musings) at 6:30 a.m.

while negotiating interstate six lane weavings

as the sun rises.

When body and mind are finally—

sufficiently still

with pen and paper,

capturing some transient glimmer seems lost.

Sad inquiry: *What was that wondrous phrase?*

Mentors have warned, *write it down,*

carry a notebook, write while driving,

dictate it, tape it, type it, compute it, compose it.

Somewhere, while I sing hymns and prayers

for mercy and forgiveness and pray

not to harm any child,

no matter how belligerent the invitation,

the poetry wanes.

I breathe. I seek higher counsel.

The copy machine is broken again.

no test today of *a) b) c) d)* or all.

this day you must write a complete paragraph,

several sentences, *yes,* and punctuation, *yes.*

The students' groans and cheers ignored equally fifty minutes
gone

end bell—tardy bell—late bell—Hurrah bell.

Bells bells bells

we will read Edgar Allan Poe.

we will consider a man named Fortunato, so unlucky a figure.

We will ask who is sane?

who is psychotic?

Is it possible to be both—at the same time?

We will note he is a fool

in motley garb, inebriated (*yes,* drunk).

Later, I will drive *assiduously* (*yes,* new vocabulary word)

on that major highway in the dark,

then sleep

perhaps to dream

perhaps to write—with impunity.

KELLY MATSUURA is an avid short story writer, with a focus on fantasy, horror, and literary fiction.

She has published works with Black Hare Press, *Sirens Call Ezine, 100-foot Crow* , Ravens Quoth Press, *Metastellar*, and many more.

Kelly lives in Nagoya, Japan with her geeky husband.

Days in Vallo di Nera

By Kelly Matsuura

Cobbled streets and fortress walls,

Sunlight dapples the brick and stone.

Tombs of hand-built houses,

Still, row by row.

A quiet peace blankets the town.

The villagers complete their work,

With goodwill and cheer.

Oh, I weep! To live this free.

But the dying geraniums,

Care not for me.

I sip my espresso. Order another,
How many partaken, soon forgotten?
Yester's meal has been consumed,
As have all delights past.
We're only to be met,
With an empty plate once more.

A soft rain falls, and I count each drop,
On my wrinkled hand.
It does no good to lament,
To recall a time long by.
One must live content, they say,
And see only the days ahead.

A youthful man would not
Stroll the plaza in gloom.
Alas, I'm not young.
I'm old and loathe my own heart.
No will to change or accept,
That life's treasures have well passed.
Nothing then, sustains me now.
Nothing now, brings joy to thee.
Have my days on Earth,
All become lost dreams?

Paper Thin

By Kelly Matsuura

Long ago, she was my light,

My world, my star, forever bright.

Then some trick, some potion or spell,

Invoked a cruel, abrupt farewell.

She left me early in the Fall,

And now we rarely meet at all.

When we do, I call to thee,

But she appears to not see me.

We don't speak, nor offer a smile.

I can't recognize her shape, her style.

Others see bright lips, blush skin,

Though to my eyes, she's paper-thin.

The sun it shines,

On her golden hair.

I try to see, I squint and stare,

Yet all I see are memories there.

I pass by her, she passes me.

Her presence feeds my misery.

We're both alone, no longer tethered.

Not to be one, 'til old and weathered.

Once the love I held all night,

Now only a mere glimmer of light.

What *is* this horrible twist?

If not one, do we each exist?

THE RAVENS QUOTH PRESS

MARC SORONDO lives with his wife and children in New York. He loves to read, and his interests range from fiction to comic books, physics to history, oceanography to cryptozoology, and just about everything in between. He's a perpetual student and occasional teacher. For more information, go to his website.

Website: MarcSorondo.com.

In the Court of the

Raven King

By Marc Sorondo

"Nevermore!" Quoth the king of night birds

> Regent of thin places
>
> Monarch of the lands between
>
> Lord of the dark places

Off fluttered weak-willed daylight birds,

> Robins, jays, and wrens
>
> In a panic fled the songbirds,
>
> Finches, ducks, and hens

The time had come for shadow business

Dark plots, murders foul

His council all nocturnal folk

The nighthawk and the owl

"The beating heart of insult," he cawed

"Maddens me with time"

"Man's retribution comes due"

"The red moon marks the time"

His armies rose high into the night

With each his gruesome task

Blood of man a perfect match

To the moon's red masque

So draped in feathers ebony

Like a midnight cloak

Mirrored eye reflecting red

Again the king bird spoke

"Nevermore," quoth that darkest of birds

Following his darkest deeds

"A new order of things has come"

"A new era that the world needs"

From the corpses and the gore

Sprouted the new day

Over all, the Raven ruled

New world from man's decay

KAY HANIFEN was born on a Friday the 13th and once lived for three months in a haunted castle. So, obviously, she had to become a horror writer. Her work has appeared in over fifty anthologies and magazines. When she's not consuming pop culture with the voraciousness of a vampire at a 24-hour blood bank, you can usually find her with her two black cats or at her website.

Website: kayhanifenauthor.wordpress.com

Evermore

By Kay Hanifen

A rose abandoned on a grave
Stolen away on raven's wings
A life haunted by the word
Nevermore

People make much of mad genius
Lonely men and their lonely deaths
Of Van Gogh's *Starry Nights* painted
Nevermore

And of your stories of grief and terror
Taken in the mystery of your death
To pick up your blood-stained pen
Nevermore

But the thing people forget is the love
Your memory and tragedy live now
By the people who kept your story alive
Forevermore

ROXANA NEGUȚ is a poet, writer, and journalist from Romania. Roxana Neguț has an impressive portfolio of writing, including books, short stories, and poetry, and her works have been published in international literary magazines and anthologies.

Website: roxananegut.com

Loneliness

By Roxana Neguț

I woke up from a moment of terrible amnesia

And looked at myself in the white mirror

I saw a face with a bitter smile

And cold eyes with gleams of steel.

I remained frozen in mute amazement

Who is that pale girl?

And what about this ephemeral body, a mere packaging,

What is my self doing inside it?

A question arises, where do I come from?

I demand an answer

What am I seeking in this barren, alien world?

Where is my serene peace?

What am I doing on this earth, between sea and sky?

Where do I come from, from heaven or hell?

I don't need a body to love

I don't need what you gave me, Creator, to live.

I don't need a heart as a mere pump.

My soul is in full agreement.

Therefore, I refuse this material gift

Which collapses after the interval of time.

I want to go back to that beloved chaos

To propagate in that eternal time.

I want to fly, to rise up to the sky

To leave this strange and lonely territory.

Let me, Lord, traverse the horizons

Throw me into eternity

Grant me my eternal loneliness.

JOHN GREY is an Australian poet, and US resident, recently published in *New World Writing, North Dakota Quarterly* and *Lost Pilots*. Latest books, *Between Two Fires, Covert* and *Memory Outside The Head* are available now. Work upcoming in *California Quarterly, Seventh Quarry, La Presa* and *Doubly Mad*.

Visiting Poe's Grave

By John Grey

In case you were wondering,

he did not rise from the grave to greet us.

We were just one more tourist bus

rumbling through the Baltimore streets,

stopping at the small church and graveyard,

emerging with cameras ready to click.

Who knows how many pull up there

for the privilege of being in the company of

Edgar Allen Poe.

Why would our rowdy lot be any different?

No ravens were about.

No pit. No pendulum.

No Roderick Usher and his sister.

And not a sign of the Red Death.

Luckily, I had my mind

to add them to the mix.

The others took a few shots

then brought out their bored faces.

I've been reading Poe

since I abandoned Dick and Jane

and their little dog, Spot.

I know the stories

like I know my own nightmares.

"You have ten minutes here,"

the guide said.

No, everyone else had ten minutes.

I had as long as I need.

JESS MARTIN is a non-binary singer/songwriter based in Western Massachusetts. They perform music in innovative collaborations. Inspired by literary artists, Jess partners with artists to co-create installations that weave poetry, puppetry and music (link below). Inspired by *The Raven*, Jess's song, "Nevermore," mines Poe's poetry for a haunting take on Lenore's story. Learn more at their website: jessmartin-music.com.

YouTube: youtu.be/fWdvRmtCLCc

Nevermore

By Jess Martin

Ravens knockin' on my door (on my door)
callin' nevermore (never ever more)
whatever did you do to sweet Lenore
Ravens knockin' on my door

Broken wings, breaking glass (break that glass)
that windows a sudden scream & crash (smash, crash)
wonder will this storm ever ever pass
Broken wings, breaking glass

Say confessions what I need (tell me what I need!)
don't repent doomed to repeat (shuffle & repeat)
this house is built on blood and greed
say confessions what I need

Raven's knocking on my bones (knockin' on my bones)

god damn bird won't leave me alone (let me atone)

some sins stay forever in my soul

raven's knocking on my bones

It's a bleak December

Down to my last dying ember

don't want to don't dare to remember

Haunted unforgiven

I loved her, loved her beyond reason

desolate, daunted, my mind's cracked open

Raven calls nevermore

it's his song I can't ignore—singin'

never more

never more

never more

never more

THE RAVENS QUOTH PRESS

PAUL BRUCKER, a marketing communications writer, lives in Mt. Prospect, IL, "Where "Friendliness is a Way of Life." He put a lid on poetry writing when he went to the Northwestern University grad ad school in a questionable attempt to learn how to think like a businessman and secure a decent income. Nevertheless, he has succumbed to writing poetry again.

Ten Minutes and Fourteen Seconds with Edgar Allan Poe

By Paul Brucker

Just because business is business

and should be done in business-like way,

because by accident I put my right foot into my left shoe,

because justice is a poor joke

and hope a promise yet to be broken,

is that sufficient reason
for the sun to depart,
absorbed by the stream
and the trunk that gave it birth,
is that sufficient reason
for darkness to fall,
and reclaim dominion over all?

That said, you must never lock in the dead
or keep them in the dark.
You must never leave the sick
until they are dead,
unable to anticipate or impair
the behaviour of other dead
and soon to be dead.

For now, if you are like me, then
you are present, reporting for duty,
two-thirds dead, maybe three-fourths dead—
requiring no difference but the ability
to savour the difference,
no ability but to distinguish
one degree of truth from another,
to take a calm, inquisitive interest in everything,

to gaze reposefully, which only begets regret
as family secrets are revealed by servants
in candlelight insufficient
to illuminate you or thwart the shadow,
the slim-legged, shovel-footed shadow
that follows and fleeces all.

When the specific quantity
of your body
is greater than the water it displaces,
the body must settle at the bottom—
it makes small difference
whether or not you love the water
or if the water is fifteen feet or five thousand feet deep.

That said, let us celebrate the stream
which flows without song from Edmonton to Enfield,
unloved stream which then flows, as best it can,
from Columbia to North Cherry,
and grows less pure, less peaceful
until a body is found,

a body that strains with all its power,

all its resources,

to produce a cry,

a cry you clearly hear and understand,

a cry you choose not to respond to, nor acknowledge.

What's peace but a set of experiences,

not something that has those experiences.

How I labour, how I toil.

How I brood, bottle and coil.

The iambic follows the Sapphic.

Slights of pen and deformities of language

sully the fair paper,

paper soon worth less

than the price paid for said paper.

How unblessed and unimportant I become, how impatient

with the efforts necessary to get the desired results

as relationships between thought and object,

subject and object, people and object,

become mere response, mere results,

the flow of blood,

not spontaneous expression or coherent view,

not a clear indication of meaning or purpose—

just a frightened head concealed from view.

I used to possess faith.

I used to believe I could manage

the distance between what is and what is desired,

what is longed for and what is long gone,

the minimum dose of a drug

necessary to produce the desired effect.

Now I see another mouse by the path,

lonely, unloved mouse,

denied a sliver of sun,

dying without sign of injury or disease

which makes no difference

because it must become

a few sticks, twigs and bones,

a little string, a little salt —

all that's left to represent religion.

Maybe that's why I'm always a step
or so behind the others, essentially left out,
unclear of purpose, of what to do or say
as the hands of menials
prepare another menial for the tomb.

Maybe that's why I always try
to apply magic, wisdom or, failing that, terror
so the language of the world—
my world—shall not perish,
though all language falls short,
all trying falls short:
an unfair exchange—
all that represents you
left under a roof full of holes,
insatiable holes that hold dominion over all.

I wear a dark moustache, scrupulously kept.
I express the symmetry of my person
with the ease and grace of my carriage,
with coat, gloves and boots
from better days
as the coffin reaches the lynch-gate
to be received in the churchyard.

I am among the people
you are among—
people to love and judge,
people to ring the bell
(nine strokes for a man, six for a woman, three for a child),
people who must show credentials
to be admitted by the agents in charge.
People who wonder, will they catch cold
if they leave their window open
(like F. Michael Vershoor waving a flag—
once divine, now deceased and despised).

Sick people who try their best to appear normal.
"That's a nice shirt you're wearing,
white as leprosy,
a nice colour for you."

I flash a hypocritical smile
and argue about trifles
in a high key with violent gestures.
I pound my fist on whatever's near at hand,
and recite jokes to divert attention
and if that fails, forge tears.

That said, even under the best of conditions,
you must watch your mind,
must observe every alteration in countenance,
and pretend to be interested,
to give a shit.

"Ahem!" someone says.
To which you reply, "aha!"
as if, by golly, we're wonderful people,
merely wonderful people, all of us, living
in a wonderful age.

See the self-centred shits with immense heads,
apparently holding many brains—
who think no good comes
unless it advances their purpose.
Where have their hands been, I wonder.
What have their hands been up to?
How can they help
with constitutional infirmities
akin to my own?

Little men eaten by the less little man,
a neighbour with teeth and claws
who despises me,
who will outlive me
unless I help him
assume the distinct look of repose
from strife and sorrow
and enter the state of absolute rest
that besets all objects,
never telling him why.

Because then, as well as now, there's no difference
between friend or foe,
no distinguishing marks or features—
merely foes that ask no longer to be
considered foes.

The best way to separate bodies
is to add a third
and the only discourse possible
is inconsistent with your objective
because the man superior in intellect
makes enemies at every turn.

And so on until there's no one left
to borrow from,
no one left
to give the benefit of doubt,
no one left to represent you.

I dread all—
marginal metaphysicians,
collywobbly clerks,
muttons dressed as lamb—
for none is so weak as me.

I dread the trumpet-tongued,
bedevilled in books,
with enough hardihood to share
his heart laid bare.

Maybe that's why I inspire hard looks,
snide remarks,
indications I've been written off.

For now, will you be so good
as to send me a copy
of the history of Tacitus—
it's a small volume,
also some soap.

In the quivering of a leaf,
a blade of grass,
a gleaming of dewdrop or hue,
walk with me,
feel the wind mingle with your breath.

Walk where the paths narrow,
and grow more intricate,
past the kindly, protective elms
and the wisp of willows
where a fox or hare hides
because it hides his scent
from the hounds.

Walk among shadows,
open your eyes in the dark,
decide which shadow to trust,
which to follow, which to fear.

Sky fretted ceiling adorned with gold.
Grass, short, springy, sweet-scented.
You, the most desirable one
in terms of look, smell and carriage,
possessed of every possible charm.

A well-shaped slender figure, noble head
so fine in proportion and expression,
with grace of step, rustle of robes
slivery-silken, with eyes of purple and pearl,
pervaded by a dim, religious light.

Nevertheless, your hands—too large,
not as beautifully formed,
nor as clean as I wish.

One touch to heal,
one to destroy.

An interesting spot
where your mouth used to be.

I'll pay twelve dollars for the furniture,
two for each embrace.

But what does it matter
when all that represents you
will r longer be you?

For so long, I fought and swore
not to sell myself
for less than my asking price,
for less than I paid.

So what if I cannot handle
or deserve my misfortune?
So what if I pass from sipper to tippler,
from gulper to guzzler?

If you remove false judgment,
there is no other judgment.
Fine wine turns bad in an unopened bottle
and what you think
is more important that what you know.

Just because my shoes grow more shoddy,
too tight and out of style,
because no one hears me,
understands me or cares,
because death renders us all alike,
is that sufficient reason

for the intensity of the beam to vary

as the square of the two planes of transmission,

is that sufficient reason

for someone, perhaps *you,*

to laze or linger

over the ground

where my grave will be.

That said or as good as said,

blame not your feet, the earth

and the ensuing silence

for they must sound like feet, earth

and ensuing silence.

For now, do me a favour.

Breathe evenly and deeply into this moment.

Pretend there has never been a better moment.

Pretend now, at last, no one can harm us.

Now, at last, we cannot harm ourselves.

**First Published in Borderline,
2012**

LYNN WHITE lives in north Wales. Her work is influenced by issues of social justice and events, places and people she has known or imagined. She is especially interested in exploring the boundaries of dream, fantasy and reality. She has been nominated for a Pushcart Prize, Best of the Net and a Rhysling Award.

Website: lynnwhitepoetry.blogspot.com

Ravens Can't Read

By Lynn White

"That's quite a raven,"

thought Poe

looking

down.

But of course

it needed to be large

to collect

up

all the pages

all the words

he had written.

And then,

what then,

what will happen next

when

all those words

are collected up

and made ready

to be consumed

for Evermore.

Ravens can't read

after all.

**First published in Ekphrastic Review,
Stef Rocknak Challenge, January 2023**

FARIEL SHAFEE studied physics. However, she loves to write and paint. Her writing has been accepted by *34 Orchard, Frisson, Parabnormal* and various Black Hare Press anthologies among others.

Website: http://fshafee.wixsite.com/farielsart

The Purgatory

By Fariel Shafee

Between heaven and hell,

I am suspended in this

nameless planet painted red

with my own

penitence.

Nothing changes here.

The end of time is its

own beginning. The air stands

still like an all

devouring

infinitum, an invisible

prison.

How the sameness of

the soil

mocks me with its steely

resolve,

drives me

mad! How long

should I have to weep, flail my own

existence

with the plea for

death until

I escape my

purgatory?

The Shadows

By Fariel Shafee

Moonlight

slowly devours the

elongated

shadows

hanging from the

clothesline, as

tears float into clouds, as the

moaning of the

damned

dissipates with the

nightly songs of the

crickets.

A pair of fiery eyes

glow, tearing up the

veil of

secret oblivion.

The bird has seen it all.

It knows all.

But it perches upon the

wrinkled tales of the

past that guard the rotting

bodies now hidden under

the dust, and then

flies away

solemnly.

The Undead

By Fariel Shafee

The ghost that came

to haunt

was not a

dead that refused

to go, but a life

buried in

stealth, deeds that

did not

wash away with the

roaring storm.

There she was, all bloody,

all muddy,

raised now

from a dusty grave too

shallow to

hold my sins.

Her eyes, filled with

pain still,

sparkled with

her hatred. Her fingers,

scarred and scratched,

still pointed straight at me.

The fire in her soul that

the maggots did not

eat up shall

tonight

swallow this

house of

lusts.

Death

By Fariel Shafee

Death is

Oozing red, festering chrome

And ice-cold blue—

Colours of the rainbow

Stripped down into

Patches.

It crawls in through

The space

Below

The bolted door, and

Lurks quietly in the

Nook, watches

Surreptitiously

Like a pitch black crow.

Death

Walks in boldly

To the

Masquerade of

Life, like

Any other stranger

Behind the grotesque

masks. Then it

Dances with you

Nightlong, until

You lie

All cold, until

Silence

Reigns.

The Eternal Ghosts

By Fariel Shafee

Yesterday marches

towards

today, and today then becomes

the past like the rolling waves of the

sea that eats away the shapeless

hills.

Nothing much

else happens in this

world that reeks of

death.

Did you see the shadows in

twilight

That tease?

Did you find the

pieces

of the raven

that was murdered by its mates

when you touched the bird

intentionally?

The ghosts trapped here

don't speak.

They just sigh

and spread out

Towards a

nothingness that

never ends.

The Wait

By Fariel Shafee

How does it feel

to wait for death

frozen

to a point?

There was something in

that buried

room of

secrets we had

to find, something

we did not

know of but

something that teased

our primal

needs to

conquer all.

How we had travelled

through the narrow paths

into

the guts of

ferocious monsters that

mocked our

pride!

We cannot move

like those little bugs

stuck inside a

spider's web, whose

screams

only muffle inside

their

own mouths.

Something watches us

cautiously, slyly, hungrily.

Something pervades the space.

The gluey sap on the floor

is the fire that eats us

slowly, dissolves our skin,

numbs us.

Something burns inside our

heads.

Something moves closer to us in

the darkness.

Darkness fills our voids.

Something causes time to

stop, almost, so we

feel nothingness

consuming us

sarcastically.

At Sundown

By Fariel Shafee

When the

Last remains of

Light drizzle into

Oblivion at

Sundown, I want to

Lie still, dream

Of yet another

Beginning.

But that's when

You come back. You

Float sparkling here

And there like a

Lightweight veil

Of cobweb that

Does not let you

See clearly into the

Nook where a

Monster waits.

You did not

Die. I did not

Clean you up

Like those

Bloodstains.

One day, I will

Fall in through a hole

Into a well that

Leads to

Nowhere, where

I shall scream

Perpetually, where

A pitch-black crow shall

Watch me like

It did

The day I

Drowned your body.

MORGAN CHALFANT is a writer, poet, gamer, and an instructor of writing at Fort Hays State University. He is a native of Hill City, Kansas. He is the author of the urban fantasy novel, *Ghosts of Glory*. You can find him on Instagram.

Instagram: @eyesonly34

Sepulchre Sirens

By Morgan Chalfant

There's a siren in my sepulchre

her voice tells me I've died for sure.

Songs soothe, rhythms resonate,

reminding me it's too late

to change what has come to pass.

Death is standing by the graveyard gate

with the sign: *You Can't Fight Fate.*

Shouting, "Your time is near!" at passersby,

and none of them wonder why,

unaware of their own demise.

Wrought iron holds the ghosts at bay,

prison bars where the dead men lay,

Wight wardens wane, sentries disappear,

at dusk when the moon appears,

ghosts gripe, "I don't belong here!"

Spectres speak with a reverence

for all living outside the fence.

Hollow men in their hallowed beds,

Raising their undead heads

To shout, "You don't deserve life!"

The siren at my sepulchre

sings with a voice too pure.

It echoes through from the other side,

Sorrow-filled for one who has died,

a black dress, one-day bride.

DAWNE LEIKER is a former journalist and native of western Kansas. She is the author of two collections of poetry, including *Death of the Civic Minded Man* (self-published) and *what remains* (Spartan Press, 2022). Her work has appeared in *Coffin Bell, Moving Force Journal, Liquid Imagination*, and other publications.

Website: liquidimagination.silverpen.org/article/raggedy-girl

The Imp

By Dawne Leiker

*We stand upon the brink of a **precipice**. We peer into the **abyss**—we grow sick and dizzy. Our first impulse is to shrink away from the danger. Unaccountably, we remain...it is but a thought, although a fearful one, and one which chills the very **marrow** of our **bones** with the fierceness of the delight of its horror. It is merely the idea of what would be our sensations during the sweeping precipitancy of a fall from such a height...for this very cause do we now the most vividly desire it—*

-The Imp of the Perverse by Edgar Alan Poe

In the faded photo, my brother smiles

a worried smile. Dirt-caked feet

betraying his ever-shoelessness.

While I, sleepy-eyed, bewildered,

stare into the camera. Unaware

of the Imp of the Perverse hovering behind me.

Till now.

Last night, I dreamed the imp returned.

He inched his way out of the dim photo.

Plunked at my feet, eyebrows raised,

and saw that I no longer wore footie pyjamas.

Then rubbed his eyes at the sight of my grey hair.

"As it is," Poe said.

"You will easily perceive that I am one

of the many uncounted victims of

the Imp of the Perverse."

"Ah," I say to the imp. "As it is.

And always has been."

It was he who lit the match

that burned my cheeks with shame.

He who squeezed and squeezed

Until my lungs clenched.

"Does it pain you to know I haven't leapt

from the brink of the precipice?" I ask him.

"Nor tossed my babies in a raging river?"

He doesn't reply—just straightens

his painted-on bow tie

and climbs upon my back.

Where he remains.

Glowing when he sparks my demented thoughts.

Edging screams to my throat during dusty sermons.

Urging the accelerator as I near a red light.

Silly little man from the garden of dismal flowers.

I paint his grin on my own lips.

Close my eyes and feel the dizzying expanse.

Knowing that, he yawns and scratches.

Waiting, always, for me to jump.

MAGGIE D. BRACE, a life-long denizen of Maryland, teacher, gardener, basketball player and author attended St. Mary's College, where she met her soulmate, and Loyola University, Maryland. She has written '*Tis Himself: The Tale of Finn MacCool* and *Grammy's Glasses*, and has multiple short works and poems in various anthologies. She remains a humble scrivener and avid reader.

Soporific Nocturnal Ramblings

By Maggie D. Brace

Soporific nocturnal ramblings lead me astray as I become an unsuspecting agent. I have become something innate yet powerful in this wakeful sleep.

Sensing the oblivion I still slumber in, I haul myself on leaden feet towards wakefulness. Pushing aside the false images that fill my brain, I slog onward to an unknown end.

Strident screeches rend the air, yet garbled speech is all I can muster in reply. Coiling upon itself, the creature before me hisses, spits venom, and slowly enrobes me in its powerful grasp. Feeling the pain and pressure, I ineffectively struggle to push its massive weight off my chest.

In a cruel twist, I become the monster myself. Seeing through its pupil slits, I spy my younger self the victim. Feeling its power and urgency, I crush all life from the puny child in front of me, and slowly encompass and devour it.

Have I become the very horror of my own nightmares? Or have I chosen another victim in my stead?

Only time will tell if I live to wake from this night, how I will emerge. Victim? Hero? Villain?

CORINNE POLLARD is a disabled UK horror and dark fantasy writer, published in Black Hare Press, Carnage House Publishing, Three Cousins Publishing, The Ravens Quoth Press, Raven Tale Publishing, A Coup of Owls Press, and *The Stygian Lepus*. Follow her dark world on Twitter, Threads, and Instagram: @CorinnePWriter.

The Feather

By Corinne Pollard

Oft I wander the night-lit world

with my mind inflicted and curled,

eluding the sweetness of sleep

and the vision of She who weeps—

She who lurks beneath my daydreams

and whispers "nothing as it seems."

Naked upon my feet, I cross

shadows and shades, swirling in loss,

and stare inside the bloody bath.

She slumbers, a razor aftermath,

pale, leaking life into dreams,

while deeming "nothing as it seems."

Her blood pools and flickers, alive

between blinks, enduring to thrive

For my sake, for every tear shed.

Return her unbroken to bed

where She giggles amongst her dreams

forgetting "nothing as it seems."

My weighted soul wishes for death,

and I stare at my selfish breath.

Why must She slumber without me?

How will She ever be set free?

Her agonal gasp lies in dreams,

taunting me, "nothing as it seems."

My fingers stroke silk, soft as lips,

and the faintness of her kiss drips

along my flesh, thawing the ice

I had sought out for paradise.

Instead, I sought the silk of dreams,

wondering, "nothing as it seems."

I blink, flickering death away,

daring to hope, daring to sway,

and daring to dream without doubt.

An ebony feather cries out

between my fingers, a night-dream

inquiring, "nothing as it seems."

Its deep darkness captures and chains

the razor pressed against my veins.

It flutters and caresses air.

My thoughts flitter without a care.

It had wandered across the dreams

unearthing, "nothing as it seems."

Unloved

By Corinne Pollard

From the pale womb, I have not been

desired like others were, nor seen

throughout my youth while others blaze—

Is it like the sun beaming its rays—

Now too hot to handle and clean,

the seed is planted, growing green,

as others sunbath, blooming smiles.

Their lives have no miserable trials,

having been spared the bloody scene.

From the bottle, I'm still unseen,

a ghost living, until I scream,

"I exist too and I'm no dream."

Their eyes scan, then fade me away,

but, for a second, I sprout grey.

I'll scream until the angels weep

or demons grant me eternal sleep.

CARMEN BOULDIN works as an English teacher. In her spare time, she writes mysteries and poetry. Her poem, "The Raven's Mourning," was nominated for a Saturday Visitor Award in 2020. She also cohosts a podcast, *The Six Degrees of Edgar A. Poe*, where they discuss Poe's influences on multiple genres.

Website: thequotableraven.com

The Raven's Mourning

By Carmen Bouldin

Gliding through the air over miles

Makes me smile since it's been a while.

One-hundred sixty-nine count I—

The years to wait, and the years to lie.

Dampening misty clouds, I soar

To prove the lore for which I bore.

Creeping up from darkness, my grave

Where I've been sworn a summoned slave.

Oh, my poet, will he waken?

I shan't wait; oh, my soul is akin!

Curiously cut—life strangled short.

Still asked: was it madness or port?

Oh, only living forty years,

I cried more than a million tears!

If I only could write again

    To explain my death to my friends.

Landing on the hard stone I seek,

Pecking as a knock with my beak.

    Familiar sounds doth come to free

    Now stirring as if luring me.

Come forth to fill my life with words

For your waiting, sad, lonely bird.

    With a pen and pondering brain

    For you now, I will go insane.

Scratching on the stone of his grave,

He wrote one word, seeming depraved.

    The raven bowed his head content

    As the poet's pen did relent.

Thank you, sir, for the writings poured.

It's my time to be "Nevermore."

    I go now to a restful sleep

    My secret not hidden or deep.

Once upon a dark moon rising,

One may see a raven flying

O'er the grave, his poet dear,

To protect his soul with no fear.

BOB BRADSHAW is recently retired and listening to the Stones and Beatles. Mick may not be gathering moss, but Bob is. He is searching for the perfect hammock to spend retirement in. His poetry has been published on the net for many years, including at *Autumn Sky Poetry DAILY, Dodging the Rain, Eclectica, Ekphrastic Review, Sea to Sky Review* and many other publications.

Edgar Allan Poe

By Bob Bradshaw

He would recall Virginia

—his child bride—years into their marriage

gazing at him like a gosling

sighting her first moon…

When that first small drop of blood

quivered on her lower lip—

her fingers trembling

out another note

on the piano Edgar

had taught her how to play—

Edgar withheld the truth,

saying "It's only a ruptured

capillary." He had tutored

his wife as well on geometry

and astronomy,

the two together following

the slow movements of stars

as if they too had all

the time in the world,

for Virginia to grow up.

For years her health

would re-bloom for weeks

only to fail once more,

like a short spring.

His hands jittery,

his grief as raw as any whiskey,

he stroked her hair, limp with sweat.

He nursed her day and night,

and became a candle on a small table,

a vigilant, faltering flame—

blood spotting Virginia's

white bed cover.

Recalling his mother's

early death—

while Virginia's fingers

grasped his in those last hours—

Edgar knew what he

had tried to ignore for years…

those he loved would always

let go, leaving him

behind

First Published *Ekphrastic Review*,
May 2020

BLACK WIDOW, aka Black Widow, is a spoken word artist from Franklin, TN. Creator of The Prodigal Poets Poetry Collective. Author of *Kaleidoscope & Poets United*, which can be found at retailers nationwide.

Her writings are of love, loss, strength & resilience; about overcoming deaths, beating cancer, and domestic violence.

Instagram: @blackwidowpoet

Skeletons

By Black Widow

Cracking the door open

Shadows seeping out

Haunted hidden past

flowing throughout

Sharp edges that may cut

Scared Echoes

making sounds

Just floating around

Trying to shout

Dust collected

from broken skin

Stepped on a shard of glass

Old blood stains

Torn apart from the inside out

Carvings on the door

broken nails

scratches in the floor

previously terrified

I made it out of there

No longer scared

Of these Skeletons

in my closet

DALE PARNELL lives in Staffordshire, England, with his wife and their imaginary dog, Moriarty. Dale is featured in over fifty excellent anthologies, pamphlets and magazines, from a variety of independent publishers, and his debut novel, *PYR*, a science-fiction space opera, is available now.

Instagram: @shortfictionauthor

Silence, Memory, and Time

By Dale Parnell

The evening cracked

with thunderous dread,

as diamond spears razed overhead,

in ink-spilled sky the tempest raged

to hear the news that you had died.

Word you had passed came with the rain,

a thousand teardrops sent to frame

the last thoughts of a haunted mind

and so, with door ajar and all my life's worth left

to rob and ruin

I walked,

unto the edge of all I knew

and found

a kingdom lost,

long hidden from the world in idle grey

wherein I saw

atop a mountain; tall and old,

inside a palace; empty and cold,

upon their thrones of blackened gold,

Lords Silence,

Memory,

and Time.

Lord Silence watched

with hanging eye

and wondered how it was that I

had come to stand before them all,

and so my story,

and so my fall,

from a place once warm and sure

now nought but emptiness and pain,

an ache that lingers, still remains,

and dulls all feelings at the root

till all my thoughts return

to a village; quiet and cold,

inside a churchyard; empty and old,

upon the marble black as coal,

chiselled with each graven letter

of her blessed name.

Lord Time;

a slender, stern and stoic gent,

had not the patience,

nor the bent

to pay a common man much heed,

and listened only in the pause

it took to take his leave.

For Time is cruel

and shows no grace,

no gentle smile upon his face,

and Time lays claim to all he sees

from that palace; empty and cold,

atop a tower; weathered and old,

in curtained chambers; crimson and gold,

and Time will see the stars die out

before his will ignored.

It was Lord Memory

who beckoned me near,

and listened with a practised ear

to every note

my heart's lament.

For all the days we would not be,

would never live,

would never see,

and all the light within that shone

extinguished, now that she was gone.

And with a sad bow of his head,

Lord Memory offered up a bed,

and come the morning, must decide

if I should live out there alone,

or evermore call this place home

atop a mountain; tall and old,

inside a palace; empty and cold,

before their thrones of blackened gold

to serve my masters;

Lord Silence,

Memory,

and Time.

TRISHA LEIGH SHUFELT Trisha Leigh Shufelt is an award-winning poet/artist. Her style is confessional poetry with emphasis on descriptive, gothic imagery. She's authored several poetry books, including *The Ghosts of Nevermore*, winner of a 2023 Saturday Visiter Award from the Edgar Allan Poe House and Museum in Baltimore, MD.

Website: artinsoul.org

The Magic of Words

By Trisha Leigh Shufelt

What if our words were spells **we**

cast, whispers we **gave**

weight without worry, writings wished upon **the**

stars who, through divine alchemy, coalesced a **future**

where all our dreams come true? We dare **to**

dream and imagine but believe **the**

impossible isn't probable. We cast doubt to the **winds**.

Yet the winds are listening, **and**

the moon watches in her glow. What if we **slumbered**

in peaceful reassurance and **tranquility**,

believed the unseen was in magical motion, and trusted **in** our abilities to conjure resplendent results? Oh, **the**

mystery of manifestation is **present**

and alive, **weaving**

wonderful worlds into **the**

unknown, waking **dull**

moments—a **world**

of pure magic is **around**

us, flowing and ebbing within **us.**

If only we could step beyond what we see and **into**

the possibility of our **dreams**.

The Mystery of Marie Roget 1842

**First Published Unearthing Nevermore-
Golden Shovel Poetry
Inspired by Edgar Allan Poe, March 2024**

All the World's a

Stage

By Trisha Leigh Shufelt

I've often wondered if this life **is**

a cosmic hat containing **all**

our dominant thoughts. Are **we**

weaving its threads into what we **see**?

Are we wearing our illusions as a collective, **or**

have we Hatters gone mad? While it may **seem**

that life is a game of chance— **a**

role of the dice. Perhaps Fate controls the **dream.**

She's a magician manifesting the madness, and **within**

her matrix, our *misery is manifold*, revealed through **a**

trick where nothing exists but the illusion of her **dream.**

A Dream Within a Dream 1849, Berenice 1835

**First Published Unearthing Nevermore-
Golden Shovel Poetry
Inspired by Edgar Allan Poe, March 2024**

The Weight of Wine

By Trisha Leigh Shufelt

Eight ounces in my right hand. **I**

take a drink. Now, seven remain. I **intend**

to finish the entire glass, which will lead **to**

another where the weight of contents will not be **put**

in my belly but in my thoughts—**up**

where eight ounces feel like eight tons. And **with**

it, others will join the party, fat and loathing with **nothing**

left to lose except Sanity. **That**

lithe lady left long ago, and **I**

imagine she is happier now that she **can**

surface above the contents that only **put**

anchors on her to pull her **down**.

Letter to J. Beauchamp Jones 1839

First Published Unearthing Nevermore
Golden Shovel Poetry
Inspired by Edgar Allan Poe, March 2024

ANN MARIE ELEAZER has always considered herself to be a bit ancient, haunted and rather otherworldly. She is someone who enjoys enchanted flights through dark fairy tales and magical places she's been drawn to since childhood. A mother of two, Ann Marie enjoys quiet time at home with her family; thrifting and long walks in the woods.

Facebook: @shesmagicandmidnightlace

Strange Lands

By Ann Marie Eleazer

Tell me of your dreams.

The ones where his heart weeps and the beauty sleeps.

But you and I prowl through strange lands of magic and mischief,

making love, dark poetry and promises we pray to keep.

Tell me of your secrets.

The ones where the wolves obey and the words escape.

But you and I find our way

through wild woodlands, half lit streets and cloudy days.

Dark Love

By Ann Marie Eleazer

I was the girl who played house in cloudy castles.

I shared secrets with crows.

And while my mother read to me happily ever after,

I dreamt of kingdoms by the sea

and the dark love of Poe.

Never much for fairytales, but dark prose I could do.

Tracing my fingertips along ghastly impressions left by the poets
we loved the most.

What I Crave

By Ann Marie Eleazer

It's not the Disney ever after magic I crave.

It's darkness and solitary moors,

crooked trees and creaking doors.

Maybe the way my heart aches and my words soar.

The ravens reciting nevermore

and the way his dark mind winks at mine.

ASHLEY O'KEEFE is from South Wales. He has two solo books: *Within The Past: Poems of Merthyr* and *Inspirations: Poetry of Pictures*, and eight collaborative books (the Rhianno & Asley Series) with the amazingly talented, Rhiannon Owens.

He's been published in various anthologies and e-zines, and is the resident featured poet on the radio show *Drive 105FM* in Northern Ireland.

Facebook: @RhiannoAsleyPoetry

Echoes from the Past

By Ashley O'Keefe

A whisper on the wind

Echoes from the past,

A raven spreads its wings

Time has gone too fast,

The clock upon the wall

Books along the shelf,

A pendulum rhythmically ticking

Suffering mental health,

Battling inner demons

A cousin for a wife,

Visual hallucinations

Addictions throughout his life,

The raven spreads its wings

Time has gone too fast...

Whispers on the wind

An echo from the past...

Pendulum

By Ashley O'Keefe

Creaking...taut...swinging...
A pendulum swings,
Its blade...sharply...glistens...
An angry rope sings,

Fear fills the room
Feel that blood-gurgling chill,
Pain creeping closer
Before death has her spill,

Creaking...taut...swinging...
An angry rope sings,
Its blade...sharply...glistens...
The pendulum swings.

The Red Death

By Ashley O'Keefe

Fatal...hideous...

Devastation...unseen...

The "Red Death"

The pestilence

Blood's redness, unforeseen...

Sharp pains, sudden dizziness

Profuse bleeding from the pores

Scarlet stains upon the body

Within half an hour, dead...without sores...

...Happy and dauntless

Sagacious was the Prince,

Prospero and his followers

Lived in deep seclusion, long since,

Within a castellated abbey

With neither ingress nor egress,

Iron gates welded

Amply provisioned, masquerade dress,

Prince Prospero provided pleasure

Dancers, musicians, beauty and wine,

Outside the walls

The "Red Death" in its prime,

Prince Prospero entertained

A most magnificent masked ball,

A voluptuous scene

In the tapestry filled hall,

Braziers of fire

Illuminated the room,

A gigantic clock of ebony

Its pendulum, swinging doom,

The sounding of midnight

Twelve strokes of the clock,

The presence of a masked stranger

Revellers whisper, in shock,

Gaunt and shrouded

From head to toe,

In the habiliments of the grave

Countenance concealed by this foe,

Dabbled in blood

Sprinkled scarlet horror,

Both vesture and mask

The Red Death terror,

Stalking the land

Now amongst the revel,

Prince Prospero shuddered

Seeing this spectral devil,

Fatal...hideous...

Devastation...unseen...

The "Red Death"
The pestilence

Blood's redness, unforeseen...

Sharp pains, sudden dizziness
Profuse bleeding from the pores

Scarlet stains upon their bodies
Within half an hour, dead...without sores...

Braziers of fire
Extinguished in the room,
A gigantic clock of ebony
Its pendulum, swinging doom.

RHIANNON OWENS moved to Merthyr Tydfil after bagging herself a handsome Welsh boy, Nicholas. She loves her cat, her mid-life crisis dresses and making her chaotic garden look even worse. Rhiannon has had eight poetry books published along with the super talented Ashley O'Keefe, and has been featured in several anthologies. Her book of bird poetry *Quills* is available now.

Facebook: @RhiannoAsleyPoetry

Taxidermy

By Rhiannon Owens

I lie abed in this quaint little inn, as lightning illuminates the room to distant thunder's grumbling,

and all I can think of is the 'trophy' cabinet downstairs

that spotted wildcat in its taxidermied stasis

and might it (please!) be my imagination, or do I hear a deep throaty rumbling?

Oh God! Is that the velveteen rub of silken fur?

A determined tap of firm, playful paw?

The solicitation of a sinister purr...prior to the hearty swipe of scimitar claw?

Beads of sweat drip down my face, as I imagine a waft of meaty breath,

tickling whiskers and fuzzy-felt ears

are you crouching on all fours, tail swishing as I strain to hear?

A hiss...a roar

I roar... I scream...

I'm in terror, shaken to the core...

Oh, please let this fearsome fuzzy feline be a conjuration of my mind,

nothing more than a twisted demonic dream

...for its ferocious maw is trapped in a glass dome

and yet...is the creature really as inert as it seems...?

Nevermore!

By Rhiannon Owens

Nevermore to suffocate in this Oblong Box

bricked up in the walls of my mind

Nevermore that tapping at my door

that plucks my fraught nerves deep inside

Nevermore to Fall like a House of cards,

no malevolent Black Cat shall I find

(and no more that Masque of Red

shall make a Morgue of my own kind...)

Nevermore shall a Raven quoth

nor from that vulture eye need I hide

Nevermore shall that Tell-Tale Heart

drum out my secrets and lies

Nevermore as that Pendulum swings,

sunken into this Pit; I'm so tired

Nevermore to pass those childhood hours

my loneliness echoed by my dreams inside

Nevermore those mocking grains of sand

evading me as they sift and slide

Nevermore, Lenore!

I await your return,

far too young you died...

"Nevermore! Nevermore! My sweetest, Lenore!"

(who I love and abhor)

I can't live without my bride...

The Bells

By Rhiannon Owens

(Then came the big freeze...)

Bodies slumped, then stiffened,

Amongst trees so rigid

I had come to seek penance,

I exhaled in relief, my breath an icicle puff

My frozen heart; the sluggish flow in my veins...

Frigid,

Yet still I fancied I heard

The ringing of the bells,

but what deathly hand might grip frosted ropes

What hellish, blue-flamed claw might encircle my throat?

The bells... The bells

Echoing amongst smothered evergreens,

The bells... weighing down my mind

An avalanche of snow,

Pine needles scattered as my thoughts fragmented.

I had come to seek penance

Alone, in a mummified world,

Where my eyelashes are ice brittle

and an infernal white blanket, lasciviously licks over the corpses in fancy gratifying swirls,

Grotesques frozen in gargoylian parody

Gargoyles spit their petrified mockery

(Yet still)... The bells... The bells

I sought penance and found my own special hell,

Trapped in an ice cube of my own solitude

I clasp my head in my hands,

Rocking to-and-fro

To-and-fro

(I despair)...

The bells... The bells...

Splintered

Oh, penance...

Grotesques frozen in gargoylian parody

Gargoyles spit their petrified mockery

Confound those bells that ring in my brain!

That sluggish flow in my veins!

Those rigid trees!

Smothered evergreens!

(Then came the big freeze...)

About the Publisher

THE RAVENS QUOTH PRESS is a boutique publisher based in Australia, dedicated to showcasing the best of international poetry craft in beautifully presented publications.

Follow us: linktr.ee/TheRavensQuothPress